THE LIBERAL MIND OF JOHN MORLEY

PUBLISHED WITH THE AID OF THE
CHARLES PHELPS TAFT MEMORIAL FUND

THE LIBERAL MIND
OF JOHN MORLEY

By Warren Staebler

PRINCETON
PRINCETON UNIVERSITY PRESS
FOR UNIVERSITY OF CINCINNATI
1943

WITH TREPIDATION,
TO THE
SHADE OF JOHN MORLEY

PREFACE

THE purpose of this book is to disclose something of the mind of John Morley—to set down the leading ideas which occupied and actuated him, and to reveal the individual temper which colored the expression of them. Since to do this satisfactorily would mean to survey, in addition to the body of Morley's published writing, his journals, notebooks, and letters, and since both distance and the terms of his will render that act impossible, this book falls short of what I should like it to be. To Mr. Francis W. Hirst's *The Early Life and Letters of John Morley* and to Mr. J. H. Morgan's *John, Viscount Morley, an Appreciation and Some Reminiscences*, invaluable for an understanding of Morley in his later life, I am, of course, deeply indebted. I have tried, however, to draw as little as possible from either of these works and to produce a study which will complement them.

"Rationalism," as Morley used the term and as it is used throughout this volume, does not mean exactly what a philosopher would take it to mean but stands, somewhat loosely, for the belief that life is understandable essentially through the operation of human intelligence, apart from any supernatural revelation. Such a rationalism, with its heavy leaning on sense perception, probably comes close to what philosophy calls empiricism.

It pleases me to thank those who have assisted me in my project: Professor Walter C. Phillips, of the University of Cincinnati, who introduced me several years ago to Morley and who has been continually sympathetic and suggestive; Professor Frank W. Chandler, also of the University of Cincinnati, and Professor Robert Almy, of Miami University, for their careful reading of the manuscript; and my wife, whose patience and co-operation through the whole enterprise are more than I can measure.

TABLE OF CONTENTS

THE LIBERAL MIND OF JOHN MORLEY

CHAPTER ONE

Formative Years (1838-1866)
A Young Man's Wisdom of Life

I

EXCEPT for a few details about his father and Blackburn, a factory town in Lancashire where he was born on December 24, 1838, there is little in John Morley's *Recollections* to help in picturing his childhood and youth. They afford only a glimpse of the bleakness of the hills about Blackburn, the starkness of its houses, and the smoke and routine of its factories. Yet it is clear that the insistence of the town on an uninterrupted succession of minutes that must count for something, on profitable employment of time—industry, in short—was stamped on him. Its "iron regularity of days and hours" was, as he admits, in no little measure related to the intellectual discipline of his productive maturity.

Something of the astringency of Blackburn pervaded Morley's home. Since his family were Evangelicals, his father, despite his love of literature and his interest in good education, adhered to the strictness of family life common to his sect. When he was forty, Morley could look back and estimate his town in *The Fortnightly Review* quite impersonally. Existence there was "dull and cramped," and its "narrow, unhistoric, and rancorous" theology did not make men love their neighbors. Yet, lean as this Evangelicalism was, it awakened and nurtured his inborn susceptibility to impassioned rhetoric. Fiery pulpit oratory gained an early hold over him, stirred up ecclesiastical longings in him; and he developed, as he afterwards confessed, an "irresistible weakness" for "the taking gift of unction." Family prayer, too, fostered a devoutness about which even in his middle age eminent contemporaries were drawn to comment; a preoccupation with what he named "holiness" and tried so frequently to define was to distinguish him until the end.

Evangelicalism left its mark in still another way. Early industrialized communities like Blackburn allowed "the most awful influx the world ever saw of furious provocatives" to moral mud-wallowing. The only attempt to stem it was on the part of Evangelical clergymen, whose firm but benevolent "moral organization" of the inhabitants made possible alone their "almost incredible" rise, between 1848 and 1878, from "something very like savagery" to self-respecting decency. Morley never forgot his early days in Lancashire Sunday schools; even after he had outgrown his belief in the Deity, he maintained the importance of the ethical system drawn from the gospels and asserted the value of "cleanliness, truth-telling, and chastity," three virtues which all Lancashireans were taught as children. The word "moral" became a dominant note in his speech.

When Morley entered Oxford, his intention was to become an Evangelical minister. Propitiously enough, his father got him settled in the very rooms in Lincoln College in which, over a century before, John Wesley had lived. And he was peculiarly aware of another coincidence—that the clergyman who had nominated Wesley to Lincoln had been named like himself, John Morley. But circumstances were not for long to conform with ambition. From that point on, both time and place conspired against him. The decade of the 'fifties was drawing to a close and the upheavals in thought of those last years, the culmination of widespread scientific investigation, were still shaking men's minds. As a result, although he continued to go and hear Bishop Wilberforce cast spells with his unction, he lost his belief, abandoned his churchly aspirations, broke with his father, and left Oxford an agnostic. This was an apostasy whose consummation probably took the bigger part of his three years at the university and yet in his *Recollections* he no more than mentions its occurrence. True, he gives considerable space to the most important works responsible for the turning of the tide at Oxford in his day, but with little comment on their effect on him, and no real tracing of his own transition. This is regrettable. Still, though an accurate chronological account of his progression cannot be made, some attention to his experience at Oxford is enlightening.

The chief forces operating on him as an undergraduate remained vital influences for the rest of his life. Classicism (that is, the wisdom of the classics), Darwinism, and Utilitarianism were powerful agents in shaping his adult attitudes. The classics did not at all mean for him what in the half-petrified Oxford curriculum of the 1850's they were for others— only superannuated Latinisms and preposterous, useless Greek myths. On the contrary, they served to liberate him, as his own judgment in *The Fortnightly Review*, almost a quarter of a century later, testifies:

... it is undeniable that some of those who have been greatest, not among "liberal politicians," but among liberating thinkers, have drawn sustenance and inspiration from classical authors. ... Liberalism in its best sense, and in so far as it is the fruit of education and thought, not the spontaneous and half accidental suggestion of contemporary requirements and events, is developed by the free play of social, moral, and political ideas; and in what literature is that play more free, more copious, more actual, more exhilarating and stimulating than in ... classical authors?[1]

It was his study of Aristotle more than of any other ancient writer, which, colored by the opinions of a thoughtful tutor, determined the stamp of his mind; he emerged from Oxford, in his own statement, an Aristotelian and not a Platonist. And Aristotelian he remained to the end of his days. With all respect

[1] Oxford's influence on Morley was ultimately one of liberation in spite of Ramsay MacDonald's assertion, "Oxford gave him nothing. The natural man pursued culture and found for him his avocation and his speech," and in spite of the fact which Mr. Hirst reveals to us, that his principles did not permit him as an undergraduate to argue in favor of relaxing the divorce laws or to commend Cobden for his contributions to politics.

for the poetic quality in Plato, he had no interest in wrestling with metaphysics, no talent for it. To one of his best friends, Frederic Harrison, he confessed in 1872: "My feelings about metaphysics are in temporary abeyance; I only know that I can't bear the unknowable."[2] In 1883, as editor of *Macmillan's*, he admitted to a contributor that for him "the metaphysics of poetry" were "not a fruitful field"; the nature of poetry did not interest him, and he added, ". . . nor would it advance our business even if we could find it out."

But what makes his acknowledgment of his allegiance to Aristotelianism doubly arresting is his further testimony, in the same sentence, that "that was the Lancastrian temperament." The soil had been sown all the time, but the seeds had lain dormant. Indeed, as an old man almost seventy-five, in speaking face to face with Blackburn citizens on the occasion of receiving the freedom of his native town, he was proud to extol the native Lancashire qualities (which he so well exemplified) of "pluck, winning frankness of speech, independence of mind, and hatred of affectation." Despite his early surrender to Evangelicalism, the dominant part of his nature was after all that which demanded earth substances, man-made materials to work with.

If the study of the classics introduced Morley to ways of thinking that were materialistic and first showed him that the true bent of his mind was one in the direction of questioning, probing, discriminating, and weighing, the influence of certain contemporary movements in thought completed the revelation. He himself has reminded us of the revolutionary works which appeared during the 1840's and 1850's. Herbert Spencer and H. T. Buckle were great forces then in stirring people to a realization of the importance of dynamic sociology and sensa-

---

[2] Throughout this book all quotations from letters between Morley and Harrison or between Morley and his sister derive from Hirst's *The Early Life and Letters of John Morley*.

tional psychology on the one hand, and the continuity of history on the other. More strictly literary were Tennyson with his "Princess" in 1847 and "In Memoriam" in 1850, and George Eliot, whose *Scenes of Clerical Life* in 1857 and *Adam Bede* in 1859 commanded Morley's attention and led to an admiration of her works that survived to the end. The fulminating Carlyle loomed across his path when a friend at Oxford acquainted him with *Sartor Resartus, The French Revolution,* and the essays on Burns and Boswell's *Johnson*, but Carlyle's influence on him did not amount to much. Undoubtedly, his preaching helped the growth of a concern with problems of society and politics, and the vehemence and color of his literary style elicited some admiration, but Carlyle's solution to England's difficulties, Morley found impracticable, and Carlyle himself not rational enough. Far more significant and consequential were Darwin and John Stuart Mill.

Just when Morley read *The Origin of Species* is not known, but since the work was published in 1859, he may have felt something of its influence during his last year at Oxford. When he began work as a journalist in London, in 1860, after leaving the university, he was already an evolutionist. And he continued to read Darwin, too, critically, if not always credulously. In March 1871, for example, as Mr. Hirst's biography shows, apropos of Darwin's *The Descent of Man and Selection in Relation to Sex*, he confessed in some agitation that "all that about ethical evolution and the Function of Natural selection in Civilization" was "very queer and doubtful." He was dismally confused in reading it but was unable to put his "finger on the fallacy." Darwin was not "at all satisfactory"; his "way of dealing with morals and society" was "as fallacious as Huxley's." Three years after this, however, his historical thinking was deeply enough imbued with Darwinian theory for him to broadcast in *The Fortnightly Review* that

Civilization on the evolutionary theory is no more artificial than Nature is artificial. It is a part of Nature, all of a piece, as has been said, with the development of the embryo or the unfolding of a flower. The modifications which our race has undergone and still undergoes are the consequences of a law that underlies the whole organic creation.

John Stuart Mill influenced Morley more deeply and lastingly than any other contemporary thinker. His *Logic* (1843), his treatise on political economy (1848), and his essays on Coleridge and Bentham left permanent impressions on the mind of the young student at Oxford, who was often seen walking, sober and contemplative, with a copy of Mill in his hand. By his own admission, it was the saintly Utilitarian who "first awoke" in him and in fellow Oxonians "that sense of truth having many mansions, and that desire and power of sympathy with the past . . . and with the value of Permanence in States, which form the reputable side of all conservatisms." In 1859 Mill's famous essay on liberty appeared, and the disciple read it with a mind ripe for its penetrating analysis. No other single volume contributed more to the composition of his Liberalism; in the *Recollections* it is considered in the same terms with Milton's *Areopagitica*.

Yet if Mill first stirred him to a conservative respect for the past, Edmund Burke was at least equally important in developing it. Exactly when he first read Burke is not known; probably it was in his late Oxford days or soon after. But, whenever it was, Burke must be considered, along with the above-mentioned influences, one of the guiding forces of his life, for much of the body of his political principle derived from the great statesman.

These influences were at work upon Morley when he left Oxford and boldly struck out for London to make a living from journalism. His first seven years there (1860-1867), a period of apprenticeship, were invaluable for a number of reasons.

First among their benefits was the experience which he

gained as a writer. He was actively employed in a number of capacities—as a collaborator with a former Oxford acquaintance; as reader for, and contributor to, the publishing house of Macmillan; as reviewer and reporter for *The Leader* (edited by the eccentric intellectual, G. H. Lewes) and the equally ephemeral *Star* and *Times*; as temporary editor of the short-lived *Literary Gazette* (1858-1862); and as reviewer and writer of middles (miscellaneous articles between editorials and reviews) for *The Saturday Review*. Such varied associations provided effective discipline for the young man who was later to have charge of one of the most influential of the large English periodicals during its fifteen greatest years. Of all the contacts, the longest lasting and the most fruitful were those with *Macmillan's* and *The Saturday Review*. Most of what he wrote in his seven trial years appeared in the columns of *The Saturday Review*, and from his industry and the happy consideration given his articles, he came to derive, so he later said, an income of seven hundred pounds a year.

The second of the benefits derived from the London apprenticeship was the establishment of friendships with three great characters who were themselves writers and thinkers—George Meredith, John Stuart Mill, and George Eliot. Morley's esteem for them found expression in written tributes. The sharpest and most beautiful of the literary portraits in the *Recollections* is that of Meredith; the review of Cross's *George Eliot's Life* (*Macmillan's*, February 1885) is an evaluation of admiration and sympathy; and the review of the *Autobiography* (*Fortnightly*, January 1874) as well as the causerie, "A Great Teacher," testifies to the veneration he had for Mill.

All three attachments owed their origin to pieces of his writing. That with Meredith, earliest formed and last broken by death, grew out of his review of *Evan Harrington* in *The Literary Gazette* for February 9, 1861. Mill, impressed by one of his "middles" called "New Ideas" in *The Saturday Review* in

October 1865, an essay designating intellectual apathy rather than antipathy as the enduring obstacle to progress, not only complimented him in a note for his "unusual amount" of valuable qualities but soon adopted him as "the young disciple" in the learned coterie gathering regularly on Sunday evenings at his house. When, in the winter of 1867, Morley made a flying visit to America, he was provided handsomely with letters of introduction written by Mill to Emerson and several other prominent men, in which he was mentioned as Mill's "particular friend." And because his article, "George Eliot's Novels," in *Macmillan's* for August 1866, praised the novelist in true Aristotelian fashion for allowing "no flapping of the wings of the transcendental angel" to be heard in her work, he found himself before long rewarded by an intimacy with her and her consort, G. H. Lewes, through the course of which he was to learn much.

More interesting, however, than the journalistic activities in which Morley was engaged, more interesting even than the formation of his notable friendships, is the intellectual development which he was undergoing between 1860 and 1867. Those were years of integration, for he was evolving an attitude toward life and the world. The distractions and hardships to which he was subjected made demands on him which he never forgot. At forty-five, for example, recalling "the dangers and risks inseparable from this dismal unbefriended apprenticeship to work" through which he had passed, he was led to make an admonition:

At no time should a young man's friends take more thought for him. Absolutely necessary it is indeed that he should learn as soon as may be to live his own life, and to walk in his own ways. But those who are bound to him may at least, in the majority of cases, secure to him some of the beautiful things of life, and ward off from him some of the ugly ones.

The record of what was going on in Morley's mind in those crucial days, he himself has left us, in two anonymous volumes,

Modern Characteristics (1865) and *Studies in Conduct* (1867), the latter of which, strangely enough, was withdrawn from sale almost immediately after its appearance. Both were collections of the best of the essays which had served originally as "middles" in *The Saturday Review*. Nevertheless, whether or not their anonymity was dictated by an absence of self-assurance about them, and in spite of the fact that in his old age he minimized their worth by insisting that no author ought to be judged by anything he had written under forty, the two books remain interesting to read, both as revelations of him and as commentaries on his times. Containing such titles as "Small Hypocrisies," "Domestic Autocracy," "Culpability and Degradation," "Occasional Cynicism," "Town and Country," and "Colloquial Fallacies," as well as such type-designations as Trimmers, Social Salamanders, Intellectual Pachyderms, and Social Troglodytes, they are related at once to the seventeenth and eighteenth centuries: to the characters of Overbury and Hall and the essays of Addison and Steele. Numerous expressions of temper, moreover, and frequent reference to Milton, Pascal, Steele, Gray, Horace Walpole, and Johnson reveal both a certain sympathy for the seventeenth century and a strong attachment to the eighteenth.[3]

The anonymous volumes have been called Morley's "Confessions." More appropriately, they are his "Books of Prejudices," for in them, inexorably critical, he is not only protesting against the fatuousness of conventional notions of things, but redefining them for himself, recasting and re-evaluating continually. Nothing is more characteristic of confession than exhibitionism

---

[3] In writing on the expansion of England in *Macmillan's* in 1884, Morley asserted that, "like most people who read the English language," he preferred "the names of the eighteenth century" to "those of all other centuries put together," attributing his preference to the fact that Macaulay's most popular essays, on shelves everywhere between Shakespeare and the Bible, were on eighteenth-century figures and treated them in a "most glowing, vivid, picturesque, and varied style."

and puerile vociferation; and there is none of that in these first
two volumes.

II

As a young man in his twenties in London, Morley was
active, ambitious, and proud. He prided himself on his intellectual vigor, for he held Socratically not only that right knowledge must precede right conduct, but that right knowledge can
be grasped only by the mind that is disciplined and vigorous.
He prided himself on his early journalistic success and justifiably felt his own superiority to "that nondescript crowd,
whose numbers" were "every day growing greater, of young
men who flock up to town to make a speedy fortune by literature." He prided himself on his realism; that is, on the honesty
and accuracy of his way of looking at life, which in after years
he was often to defend, as when in 1884 in *Macmillan's*, after
crossing the threshold of his political career, he remonstrated
with opponents for branding him a pessimist. He was not, he
protested, "unless it is to be a Pessimist to seek a foothold in
positive conditions and to insist on facing hard facts." His
realism, in true Aristotelian fashion, was an intellectual middle
ground between optimism on the one hand and pessimism on
the other, between cynicism and sentimentality. Yet it was not
compromise. It was simply that place in the perspective of the
mind's eye where the relationships among facts showed, least
distorted. Compromise, on the other hand, was a disposition to
deny, or equivocate about, the rightness of things seen, if denial
or equivocation made the discharge of daily obligations any
easier. Thus Morley, forswearing pessimists, was at the same
time indignant with sentimentalists who, looking wistfully back
on their past, idealized it as a time of unalloyed happiness and
wept over their severance from it. Still bearing the pain of the
estrangement from his father, and reconciled to his inevitable
alienation from many of his college friends, he proclaimed that

any recollection of the past was tinged with anguish and that
any attempt to relive it resulted in needless misery. Gilders of
the past and wishful recapturers of it were just such people as
imagined that prostitutes, in remembering the sweetness of their
old mothers and the innocence of their childhood days, were
sobered and incited to better conduct; he, the realist, knew that
prostitutes promptly had recourse to the solace of gin.]

As a regular contributor to *The Saturday Review* Morley
became a roving reporter on human nature-at-large, a critical
examiner, an appraiser of the times. "The prime characteristic
of the Englishman is activity and energy," he discovered, and
this he saw incarnate in the Englishman's great Empire. But
everywhere it was activity accompanied by spiritual complacency, by intellectual puerility and swagger. The aristocracy
was "bloated and effete." The middle class, dedicated to the
pursuit of money and position, was deplorably material-
minded, Philistine. Not that without reservation he condemned
the desire to become rich, for he knew that it could breed, among
other traits, industry, thrift, and foresight. But he abominated
the urge to accumulate money for its own sake. The temper of
the age, he saw regretfully, was one of selfish discreetness and
opportunism; and a prevalent British type was the trimmer, the
man, who, Polonius-like, steered a middle course, his equivocal
sails ready to bow to a profitable wind in any direction.

Apart from the engrossing activity of commerce, Morley determined to assay the secular instruction motivating middle-
class people. The stuff that fed childish minds, he perceived,
was either harsh and thorny or flabby, insipid pap. The first
diet, epitomized in books of instruction like those of Hannah
More, was dangerous because its bleakness begot only bleakness. What geniality and liveliness of mind, what warmth and
grace of temperament could be the products of sermonizings
that condemned clubs as "subversive of private virtue and
domestic happiness," racing as unnatural, croquet as wicked,

and walking in gardens on Sundays as frivolous? Equally objectionable was the other fare, found in such books as Martin Tupper's *Proverbial Philosophy*, whose dressed-up platitudes, or "sonorous inanity," produced foolishness. In addition to deforming personality, however, both diets fostered an utterly false conception of values in which conduct was invariably confused with capacity. That a boy went to church regularly, said his prayers every night, rose early every morning, saved his pennies industriously, or that he did not swear or lie to his parents or cheat his brothers and sisters—these things did not justify his neighbors in envisioning, as they inevitably did, a successful career for him, because they knew nothing of his intellectual potentialities and had never seen him subjected to a test. Mistaken for capacity was a mere docile conformity to the thinnest of conventions. "The highest conduct" could only be "the fruit of the character . . . most raised by wise intellectual culture."

Yet the times did even more damage to females in the lamentable "education" to which they were subjected and the conduct they were exhorted to follow. Morley was pained by the ignorance and inadequacy of young ladies again and again. Too often it was his misfortune, as an eligible young man in town, to have to sit through an elaborate dinner with a frivolous and stupid companion at his side, or to be trapped behind ferns at a fashionable dance in an incipient flirtation by a personable admirer to whom it was impossible even to mention Shakespeare or Burke, or to be sentenced to five long acts in a theater box with a simpering nymph who had no notion even of what "denouement" meant. Indeed, if there is one social theme in these early years to which he returns more repeatedly than to any other, always with special indignation and disdain, it is this of women and their deficiency. He may not have believed that all females *per se* were the confusion of men, but he was unmistakably convinced that, in their present state, they were a thorn in men's flesh.

The strongest expressions of his discomfiture suffered at the hands of women found their way no further than *The Saturday Review*, for they were not reprinted in either of his anonymous books. On fire after his experiences in fashionable Belgravian society, in withering contempt and sarcasm he castigated it. What he saw was a little world of pretence and deceit as glittering and false as that of Duessa's Castle of Pride in *The Faerie Queen*, in which the role of women was to attract and ensnare, and the accoutrements of fashionable life—dances, dinners, teas, croquet parties, theater groups—were nothing but the trappings of a commerce in matrimony.

But not in Belgravia alone were women stupid and inadequate. Everywhere in England they were woefully uneducated, and in the country their isolation handicapped them doubly. Still, though they were more capricious than men, though those who were called "clever" were either dull and conceited or pert and conceited, though they possessed an "overrated character for sensibility"—a quality in which men were at least their equals, though they were "very rarely magnanimous" because "magnanimity is not a feminine virtue," and though they were not, as a rule, thoughtful readers and were "so intensely practical, in the narrowest and often the worst, sense of the term, as to look with habitual distrust upon those general ideas which it is the chief business of literature to sow," still Morley acknowledged that women sometimes revealed "a full-blooded sweetness of character . . . worth more than mere intellectual quickness." And even "the ordinary girl," he conceded, was "not morally pachydermatous." She was very often "uncommonly dull and stupid and silly, but the dullest and stupidest may be the most sensitive about exposure and humiliation." And no English girl he had met was guilty of such extreme folly as he had recently found betrayed in print by an American female who confessed she was panting to "throw her soul into the arms of the Infinite."

Relations between men and women, in view of the nature of women and their disgracefully shoddy cultivation, concerned Morley. He decided that friendship between the sexes, although possible, was a rarity, for it occurred almost invariably late in life, and even then nearly always among illustrious French people. Love, a much stronger relationship, interested him even less. Temperamentally uninclined toward it, he was fixed in his disparagement: love may be elemental, but it is at the same time elementary. A physiological manifestation, it disrupts thinking and causes aberrations in conduct. And adopting St. Paul's terminology, he made his terse pronouncement: "When he is in love, a man may think as a child and speak as a child; but if he is to go on growing he must put away childish things."

On the subject of marriage Morley's convictions were severely realistic. He was careful never to strain the limits of human nature, never to expect too much from it. Young as he was, he knew the importance of *amour propre*. Profiting by the innumerable evidences in husbands and wives about him of a disillusioning descent from passion to indifference, he determined to save himself from the fate of a matrimonial morass. But he inveighed not alone against those who were betrayed by passion into entering a relationship whose eventualities they were too blind to foresee or too undisciplined to master. Many men he saw yielding themselves spinelessly to marriage, superstitiously accepting it as a social Rubicon, inevitably to be crossed by everybody sooner or later. Contemptible fools! As though a pusillanimous closing of the eyes and plunging into the waters of a Rubicon could make the direction of anyone's life any easier! As though there could be an instantaneous reinforcement or transformation of character, a sudden magical solving of a problem!

Unwilling to postpone "the future to the present," to purchase "a small gratification now at the sacrifice of a greater and more enduring good to come," Morley saw marriage much as Swift had seen it in his "Letter to a Young Lady." The rapture of romantic love is short-lived. In its place must come a relationship based on reasonableness and characterized by taste, good-naturedness, tolerance, and trust. Speculation about offspring led to a sardonic query: are babies, like bad port wine, a minor tribulation or a catastrophe? A child might well be a "nicer object" than a man, he conceded, but a man is better because he is useful. On the care and raising of children, nevertheless, he had considerable opinion to impart. Since for the sake of their unborn progeny, it was the moral duty of all adults to maintain good health, he advocated gymnasiums and exercise for women. He decried the prevalence of domestic autocracy and looked for the day when parents would cultivate a "discreet indifference" rather than an "unremitting attention" toward their minors. Children should be trained to be independent and the reins of parental discipline gradually slackened. A desirable system was one in which a child in his sixth or eighth year would pass from a despotic government into a monarchy with diminished centralization, from which, in turn, he would proceed when he was fifteen to a limited monarchy, arriving ultimately at a republicanism, with the one-time parent-dictator now his guide and friend.

Fortified as he was against the attractiveness of women, Morley was equally secure from the blandishments of what people called nature. Buxom breezes, azure skies, moonlit waters, downy meadows, flowers, birds—these could not seduce or distract him from his awareness of windstorms, floods, drouths, insect plagues, animal deformity, bodily disease. But it was a time of Romanticism still. The urge exemplified by Wordsworth, Byron, Keats, and Shelley had not died with their deaths; in the late 1860's in Swinburne's throat it was finding even more vociferous expression. Everywhere Morley encountered "Sympathy with Nature" and young men and women maudlin in demonstrating it. He was revolted. "Sympathy with Nature," he decided, was usually a high-sounding name for loafing on the back in the sun, not necessarily bad in itself, but "wholly unfruitful of positive results upon character." Too often, moreover, it was a hatred of man, a contempt for him—an excuse for releasing individual lusts and indulging "anarchic passions." It was to be condemned as dangerous to society; "as much civilization is due to the steady repression of nature as to its development."

"Perhaps one of the most certain signs," however, "that the true meaning of sympathy with nature" had been recognized in the 1860's, "in spite of the growth of this . . . plague-stricken school," was "the visible spread of the idea that every sentient creature ought to be treated with humanity, just as much as the members" of the human species. This "consideration for all sorts of foul animals and reptiles," along with the abandonment of the policy of "maltreating lunatics and burning ugly old women" for witches, was encouraging evidence of progress in one direction, at any rate. Morley still remembered wincingly the horror he had experienced as a child in discovering other "boys . . . pulling flies to pieces and digging the eyes out of toads." He never ceased to plead that "dumb and helpless things have a capacity for something which at least passes with them for pleasure." He satirized certain dukes who had been praised in newspapers for their duck-shooting records and he praised as evidence of Victor Hugo's great soul that incident in his *Légende des Siècles* in which a horse pulling a cart avoids stepping on a weakened toad in the road. Attached as he became, moreover, to George Eliot and G. H. Lewes, he found it almost more than he could do to call on the pair because he was habitually encountering maimed animals in the lower hall, subjects for Lewes in his laboratory experiments.

Nature was kind, then, in one act—that of implanting the

instinct of "pity in the souls of the creatures she has abandoned." And for Morley, human beings on this planet were
abandoned. He believed with Lucretius that, as one part of the
nature of things, men and women were no more than brief
manifestations of matter, living their lives on the earth utterly
unrelated to the will of an interested, guiding deity, for there
was no such deity, or, if there was, all worldly evidence pointed
against his having planned a special destiny for his creatures.
And yet, abandoned though he was, Morley could not recommend a course of licentious self-indulgence for himself. He was
too awed by the pitiableness of human life—too sensitive to its
suffering, its frustrations, its incongruities, its cosmic insignificance—to take advantage of its supernatural dissociation, its
transitoriness, and glut himself bestially. His Blackburn environment had given him a physiological repugnance to lust in
the raw; and his childhood Evangelicalism had developed in
him an intellectual abhorrence of the consequences of sensuality. Through classical literature, Lucretius in particular, he
had learned at Oxford that man can acquire, through his own
endeavor, a dignity that will give his life value. What if it is
true, he appealed, "as fiery poets of despair are never weary of
crying aloud to us, that Nature hates us, and that the gods are
never found by our prayers? Is not this all the more reason why
we should be as gods to one another?" But it was not only that
he was by nature pitying or that he conceived pity as a godlike
attribute, and it was not only that he discountenanced yielding
to lust as a smirching of dignity; as a member of a civilized
society he knew the necessity for self-restraint and discipline
among human beings.

If the idea of self-denial is to be expunged from the list of the things
worthy of cultivation, then society must inevitably fall to pieces. If all
men and women are to insist on drinking to the dregs the cup of every
desire of their animal nature, without a thought of the effects which may

flow from their gratification, then it is plain that most of the business of the world will come to a standstill.

And yet it was not enough for a man to restrict himself and abstain; a morality of negation might enable him to save his own soul but it would contribute nothing to better society. Although one's chief purpose in living was admittedly to secure his own contentment, one ought to have co-ordinate with that the desire to do everything in his power for his fellow beings. Morley had not outgrown the Golden Rule and not for nothing had he grafted it to his Utilitarian principles. "The man lives most perfectly whose constant happiness is found in the consciousness that, in doing the best that he can for himself, he is also doing the best that he can for every being that is capable of having good done to it." In deriding the conventional confusion, then, of conduct with capacity, he was not advocating a discard of conduct; he was only urging the conception of a new and broader kind. He had no hesitancy in making his stand clear. "After all, the end of everything is living," he maintained. "Conduct is at once the aim and the test of all our learning and thinking and striving." But it was this larger, more humanitarian conduct that was alone ennobling.

There can be no more deadly and baneful influence than the one which teaches men to prefer anything under the sun to the happiness of the whole mass of sentient creatures. Beauty, truth, justice, every virtue, every pursuit, every taste—they are all good because, and just in so far as, they augment this stock.

For Morley fame was the spur to achievement, and he made no secret of his desire for it. He had no patience at all with that "certain commonplace standard, easy to satisfy, beyond which nobody expects us to go," and no tolerance for self-styled "philosophers" who would "leave fame for fools" and content themselves "with listless irresolution or with truculence." Fame was a justifiable and worthy motive because it had "produced the greatest and most beneficent achievements that have made the globe as decently inhabitable as it is." The pursuit of it was in no way irreconcilable with the magnanimous conduct he had defined for himself; and the love of it, in contradistinction to Milton's pronouncement on the question, was not an infirmity in any noble mind. Morley was not a complacent Pharisee but only a self-respecting young Englishman justifiably priding himself when he observed that most young men of his own age who had come to London to make literary reputation had not stood up under the severity of journalistic competition. He knew, at twenty-six, that he had already partially succeeded in doing what he wanted to do, in translating "the obscurity of local success into the daylight of metropolitan fame."

But it was not fame as a writer that he wanted. His ultimate objective was not literature but politics. The choice between them was essentially one between thinking and doing, and he decided in favor of doing. Ever since his Oxford days the problem of establishing a preference had been on his mind. Yet he liked to think that he was acting in accord with a national tendency as well as with a personal disposition. Relating his own act to a background of national tradition gave it broader dimensions and suggested greater possibilities. "The prime characteristic of the Englishman," he had written, "is activity and energy"; so in casting his lot for "the conflicts of the political arena," he, like others before him, was gratifying "a national instinct."

"Some men," he reflected, "would rather have been the author of *Hamlet* or the *Principia* than have held the highest office in the state, but they are very often just the men of the smallest intellectual calibre and least likely to erect one of these intellectual monuments more lasting than brass." He himself would rather have delivered one of Gladstone's best speeches than have written the *System of Logic* or the *History of Inductive Philosophy*. But it was "the *highest* office in the state," or a *Gladstone*, or one of Gladstone's "*best* speeches" on which he fastened his attention; nothing less than the best in political attainment or performance was worth striving for. He confessed that a second-rate writer can do more good than a second-rate politician. There was nothing to forbid him, however, from straddling both literature and politics, from becoming at once a writer and a statesman, even though "the two characters, in their fullest measure, are not frequently combined." Burke had possessed both characters and expressed them consummately; and in his own time both Gladstone and Disraeli had gained reputations in literature as well as in government. With his eyes fixed on such pre-eminent archetypes, he would aim at the same embracing duality of achievement. At least he would use letters as a preparation for politics. How could the discipline exacted by a vigorous career as a writer be in any way inferior to the training obtained as a law student or as a member of a town administrative commission? And what better preparation for a vigorous career as writer could be had than the apprenticeship to which he was every day subjecting himself among the working thousands in London? Learning human nature as he was, and proving his ideas about life, his ultimate outlook on things would be saner as well as more comprehensive than if he were biding his time as a speculative visionary somewhere in the seclusion of a university.

Nothing is more extraordinary about Morley than the perfect and healthy confidence with which he decided on his life career and went about laying its groundwork. Knowing himself and estimating his capacities judiciously, almost infallibly, he made his plans and charted his steps coolly, deliberately. Everywhere in his evaluations he was intent on discovering, and seemed always to perceive, the proper limits of things. Thrift, for example, was not at all, though most people took it to be, "penurious frugality." It was "the wise and careful outlay of money" (how, not what, you spend), which lay between parsimony and prodigality, and it involved "a really lofty moral excellence."

Likewise, in his attention to fame, and in weighing his own abilities, he took pains to be equally discriminating: it was good to have one's eyes on great men like Pitt and Fox and Burke, but it was not good to be persistently measuring one's self alongside friends and acquaintances. Continued self-comparison of this sort bred the Pharisee and deluded people into finding their superiority in wholly adventitious traits. Tormenting and incapacitating themselves mentally, they made it impossible for magnanimity, one of the two or three most desirable intellectual traits, to find its way into their brains.

Morley early resolved that his own contribution to humanity would be made as an enlightener and reformer. He would stir people to see things as they should be seen, to free themselves from superstition, rote, cant; he would awaken them to an awareness of the conditions in which they lived and initiate campaigns for their betterment. "The first of all social responsibilities," he maintained, "is to have an intelligent set of convictions upon the problems that vex and harass society, and continually keep a wide margin of miserable anarchy about her skirts." The second was to hold those convictions strongly and propagate them. Only through an education of the public, through a spreading of information and a development of opinion, could pauperism, prostitution, and the rest of "the most terrible questions of today" be attacked and solved. It was imperative that every man be taught what he himself had cultivated—"the all-important habit of taking care that his mind works at ideas instead of allowing it to absorb their pale shadows."

Of course, men *could* be taught and civilization *could* be improved. As to that, he had made up his mind in advance; only, in his customary realistic temper, he was cautious to set limits on what he meant. "Society," he concluded, "is a machine which, though always and boundlessly susceptible of improvement, generally works for the welfare of the community as well as the age will allow." And "man," he had come to see, "is in practice not so low nor in capacity so unspeakably sublime" as Carlyle and Emerson had maintained. Here was no dreamy enthusiast, no fanatic, but a man who all his life was to maintain that truth's ground is a middle ground, and that fidelity to it, though it means a moderation or reconciliation of extremes, does not entail compromise. Acquaintances, impatient with seeing him constantly in his role of Socratic gadfly, accused him of being querulous—of venting through his social criticism nothing more than his own strong desire to go back to the opinions and customs of his grandfathers. He denied the impugnment. He wanted no regression; but no more did he will a consummating acceleration of progress. He did not believe in "an instantaneous and unimpeachable millennium," he protested, and did not want to go to one any more than "a bad little boy does to heaven."

The career of reformer is a difficult one, for apart entirely from the personal qualifications of the aspirant to it, the way in which it is pursued can make all the difference in the world between success and failure. To reform a man, you must first show him that you respect him and have faith in him. So Morley reasoned. "Contempt for public opinion" he deplored. "In by far the majority of cases," he insisted, it "is a sign either of consummate impudence or surpassing shallowness," and the man who is always intent on being "in a complacent minority of one never makes a mark" on anybody "for the sufficient reason that he has no mark particularly worth making." He could not tolerate people who made themselves different just to be "original" or daring. Although Herbert Spencer was recommending to young men the practice of responding to dinner invitations by appearing without a dress suit and wearing a long beard, his own strong conviction of the importance of regularity and conformity in the little things of life forbade him to condone such *bizarrerie* in conduct. It was more, however, than an ingrained distaste for sartorial eccentricity which led him to take issue with Spencer; it was the certainty that a flouting of the proprieties would be ruinous to him in his role of reformer. He must be circumspect and reasonable. "The identification," he wrote, "of all uncommon and unpopular views with strange manners and uncouth attire is a fatal course for anyone to pursue who wishes such views to become common and popular as speedily as may be."

The qualities needed for success in a public career, Morley had no difficulty in ascertaining as primarily intellectual, and he lost no time in cultivating them. It was not that he relied on a rigid routine, an exact budgeting of daily hours to be followed week in and week out. He was disciplined himself, but he knew that the most nearly infallible system of dams and dikes and channels in the world is worthless if there is no current for them to control. About him he saw young men by the dozens putting their faith in such abstract schedules, only to disappoint themselves and their admirers eventually by amounting to nothing. The trouble, here as in other things, was that superficial conduct was being mistaken for capacity, or adolescent enthusiasm for ability. Hardly anybody took the pains to know himself or to see beneath the surface in anybody else. Year after year, breakdowns continued to mystify both their victims and their witnesses. But they held no mystification for Morley. He had given them prolonged attention and found them perspicuous. Breakdowns occur, it was obvious, not always through vices but often because of "a whole stock of intellectual habits which, though scarcely visible in themselves, are not less pestilent in their consequences than drunkenness or incontinence or systematic idleness." We must realize that "there is all the difference between a strong passion and a strong reasonable will." What is indispensable is a "vigilant tenacity"; "men with the best aims constantly break down because they cannot bring their great minds so low as details and items and little detached bits of labour and forethought."

More important than intellectual carefulness, however, in gaining the world's really great prizes, are intellectual breadth, intrepidity, and vigor. Breadth, we have already seen, must be secured if one is to establish immunity to tormenting rancour, spite, jealousy. As for the second of the virtues, everybody admits the value of intrepidity in physical conflict and praises it; what he must learn and be willing to concede is the even greater desirableness of it in questions of thought. To be "industrious or of good morality, and decently intelligent" at twenty-five is not enough; to become a Gibbon or a Buckle or a Hallam one needs intrepidity. And intrepidity is after all a manifestation of vigor, which "is perhaps the least to be dispensed with of all those virtues of understanding . . . because conduct, which is the ultimate test of the worth of all thinking, is sure to become weak and wavering in proportion to the falling-off of this internal vigour."

These invaluable intellectual traits might well be supplemented by the incitement to be derived from two additional sources—one's own imagination, and the circumstances of English society. Imagination not only assisted in the growth of sympathetic, charitable conduct; it also, even in "castle building," was a bracer and a stimulus to young people in their ambitions—provided it was "superintended by reason and common sense." Thus arts like poetry and music could inspire young men to glorious achievement. The encouragement offered by the organization of English society, though more adventitious, was no less a stimulus. Who could resist the incentive to high endeavor afforded by the examples of Disraeli and Gladstone? Neither vast wealth nor aristocratic birth was any longer a prerequisite to the greatest political office in England. Careers were now open to talents, and a man's abilities alone should determine how far he was to climb.

Morley had nothing but scorn for those who in the face of
these circumstances desisted and paraded an attitude of sour
grapes or tried to disparage all effort by whining over the ad-
verse power of chance or fate. Breakdowns in life, visible or
invisible, "are all the result of some kind of moral worthless-
ness. Neither untoward circumstances nor the evil behavior of
others can effect the fall of a man with a firmly based character." They may slow him up or make him stumble in his
movement, but they cannot throw him into ruin. "People break
down because they do not take pains with their character, as
they would with their bodies if they were going to fight or to
run a race. They seldom keep themselves in moral training."
It was not that Morley denied the existence of chance or habit.
He felt their force well enough, but he refused to recognize that
it invalidated human free will. It is every man's duty, when his
character is building, to exert his will and see vigilantly to it
that the tastes and habits he forms are good ones; then in time
of crisis he will be more likely to act intelligently than if he has
grown up undisciplined. "Circumstances only act as a magnify-
ing instrument," he averred; one makes his character and then
is drawn along by it. This was a position from which he would
not retreat.

It is very proper and elevating to believe that "Man is man and master of
his fate." Practically this is by far the most important and the most worthy
aspect of human action, and to lose sight of this as the greatest of all principles in its kind is to suffer a complete moral paralysis. Only, in surveying
life, it is childish not to see that a man is not by any means the only master
of his fate.

One's ancestors and parents, who bequeath him a certain physiological and intellectual inheritance, and one's environment,
which modifies that inheritance, must not be forgotten. Nevertheless,

If a man has brains and health and a decently early start in the world,
there is no external clog to prevent him from rising as high as he likes.

There is nothing in the constitution of society to hinder an educated man from getting whatever praise or pudding his own qualities and conduct entitle him to.

Along with maintaining this, Morley flatly refused to condone the conduct of anybody who, in laziness or indifference, made no effort to capitalize his abilities. There were only three misfortunes—"noxious elements," he called them—that might justify a man for sinking into despondency and inactivity: disease, bereavement, and spiritual dilemma. All other circumstances were non-extenuating.

Still, even in the absence of the "noxious elements," one was not to give himself up to the sweating pursuit of an early fame. Although anybody with high capabilities and the strong desire to realize them is impatient to arrive early, he must restrain himself from falling into headlong haste. In spite of his placing a premium on intellectual vigor, Morley was no zealot. Like Milton in his early twenties, whose sonnet in reproach of Time, the subtle thief of youth, he often thought of and was fond of quoting from, he was moved by the almost irresistible urge to try his wings. He checked his eagerness, however, and reminded himself reasonably of his ultimate objective, a "large and serene internal activity" which was to be attained, not by precipitousness in youth, but only by "time and industry and the maintenance of a thoroughly open mind." For him, ripeness was all. Short cuts, he would not tolerate. And yet everywhere about him modern speed—the mechanical speed of railroad, steamship, telegraph—was deluding people in their attitude toward the affairs of life. There was already, for example, in the matter of reform too much satisfaction with talking and writing as a sure means of making human beings do what is right. Men should be always aware that there is no short and easy method to either bodily health or moral strength. Short cuts and dispatch may be all right in business, but they rub the "delicacy and bloom off life" if followed in all activities.

It is this unwillingness to sacrifice the "delicacy and bloom" of life that supplies the clue for the discovery of Morley's conception of satisfying living. Attainment of high office, while it may satisfy certain desires and consummate certain aptitudes as well as offer opportunities to do good to others, does not in itself guarantee happiness. A man must have a fruitful private life and be something in himself, apart from his public successes. He must possess "that wisdom which is the perfect and full flower of human character." This wisdom, one can see, comprises a number of important recognitions.

First and basic is the realization that one must not expect too much from life. Nothing is more destructive of any capacity to live profitably than cynicism; and in nine cases out of ten, cynicism grows most quickly from a soured and festering idealism. Again and again, Morley warned his readers in *The Saturday Review* that any inexperienced, credulous individual who adopts an immoderately altruistic attitude toward life is liable to have his ideal suddenly blasted and be sent sprawling toward the other spiritual extreme.

The second recognition is that human character reaches its full flowering only when the soil in which it is nurtured contains "certain virtues of the heart" as well as those of understanding. Thus, although in the "broad course of public transactions" it is the talents related to intellectual capacity and cultivation that count most, in domestic life and individual happiness it is the graces and moral elements that are important. "Innate shrewdness and mother wit," "gentleness and delicacy and depth of moral sympathy," "simple affectionateness," and "honest good will"—of all of these Morley could so disinterestedly see the worth that he was led to an admission about them which sounds almost like a contradiction from his lips: "It is the mark of a real highmindedness to be able to tolerate intellectual commonplace when it is accompanied by these minor virtues."

Somewhat like a corollary to this emphasis on "virtues of the heart" is the third recognition that things in themselves, apart from any visible or "actual" use of them, can be good and desirable. "I cannot praise a fugitive and cloistered virtue, unexercised and unbreathed," wrote Milton heatedly in his *Areopagitica*. "Virtue, of its very essence, is either practical or nothing," affirmed Morley. Yet, in spite of his concurrence with Milton on the subject, in spite of his aversion to the "dilettantism of virtue," he was not an extremist in the practical. Certain ideas, certain traits of mind were, after all, worth fostering as ends in themselves—apart utterly from any palpable external results. The "consciousness of integrity and highmindedness" was to be so considered. Similarly, a love of justice was invaluable for its wholesome, equilibrating effect on one's own character. Almost everybody, however, remained motivated by the age-old "headlong anxiety" to get to the end of something, to finish the task at hand, to seize what he had set his mind on attaining. How regrettable, sighed Morley, when in "the long run, we shall probably find that the exercise of the faculties has of itself been the source of a more genuine happiness than has followed the actual attainment of what the exercise was directed to procure."

The fourth recognition concerns the acceptance of the elementary fact that nobody can escape pettiness, even sordidness, in the routine of life. It is too bad that we cannot live as pure and simple and lovely a life as did Adam and Eve before the Fall. But, since golden ages and utopias are impossible, the only way in which we can compensate for their lack is through cultivating "a habit of taking vivid interest in all that is passing in the world in practical exploit and speculation and art, to give existence an air of dignity and size and grandeur." Such a universalizing interest in things is, after all, the only kind compatible with a "large and serene internal activity." So Morley, in contradistinction to intellectual Tories and those he called Social Troglodytes, did care earnestly about such matters as "the American War, or the coming Reform Bill, or Jamaica," or "whether Governor Eyre was right or wrong, whether species have their origin in natural selection or in distinct acts of creation."

In valuing the "habit of taking vivid interest in all that is passing in the world," however, and in identifying the source of "the best kind of happiness" as being "in the widest possible range of interests and tastes," Morley, who at twenty-seven was unwilling to concede that simplicity in living was more than "a negative virtue," did not lack "the keenest appreciation of all minor pleasures, and the nicest attention to all minor adornments." Indeed he was fastidious in his pursuit of them to the point of being later nicknamed "Priscilla." "The proposition that all pleasant things are right is untrue," he conceded, "but it is certainly not so radically untrue as the more popular proposition that most pleasant things are wrong." Against the current practice of prescribing long, unbroken periods of work with infrequent intervals of pleasure, he revolted. A prescription of a quart of brandy one day and a quart of water the next is not at all a prescription for a mixture of brandy and water. "If it be sound doctrine that a line every day is the secret of success in art, it is not less true that an instalment of pleasure every day is at least one of the secrets of happiness in life."

The fact that many pleasures are small did not bother him. "Life without those secondary adjuncts of grace and dignity is like one of those plain, gaunt houses which are often eminently commodious and healthy, but which still have no claim to be considered types of the most perfect domestic architecture." It was clear to him just how the widespread objection to minor pleasures was formed. People at large could see no "radical connection between dignity in small matters and genuine worth and power in . . . weightier matters" and so they arbitrarily dismissed all small matters as trivial and worthless. Since there was no relation between sitting down to dinner with clean hands and abstaining from robbing their neighbor's chicken house, why should they bother about washing their hands? For Morley, however, the absence of any such radical connection was no bar to the recognition of "dignity in non-essentials as a substantial and independent merit." Only "clowns," he said, "look on the simplest points of good breeding as despicable fopperies." For actual fopperies and small hypocrisies, he had no use; they were too often the outgrowth of extreme self-consciousness, self-uncertainty. But he was pained to think that "an absurd and offensive affectation" should ever be confused with "the genuine air and manner of distinction."

A glance at "those secondary adjuncts of grace and dignity" which Morley prized most discloses the refinement and discrimination that were to distinguish him for the rest of his life. He delighted in good living. Choice wines were dear to him, and he prided himself as a connoisseur. Knowing his clarets, he held it imperative for other men to; dullards who could not tell Gladstone from Lafitte or Cape from Port met with something hardly short of intolerance in his company. On fine foods, he was equally insistent. He had an aversion to certain "popular poisons"—to melted butter, for example, and pork, which he was aghast that people really ate; he condemned suppers at nine or nine-thirty as unhealthful perpetrations; and he dismissed the fish dinner as the "most astounding invention of modern civilization." Good painting pleased him, and he surrounded himself with specimens of it. Fond of the theater, he was even more a devotee of music—of its larger forms, the oratorio and the opera, but of its smaller forms, too, among which he was modern enough in 1865 to prize Mendelssohn lieder and Beethoven sonatas (except for their "abstrusest parts," which he left to impressionable young ladies). Preoccupied with conversation, he disciplined himself to become adept in it. Good conversation, he knew, requires art to conceal art. It does not consist of a rehashing of magazine or newspaper articles, it need not and ought not be disputatious, and it is damaged, not improved, by flashy paradoxes. At its best it is a "quiet, easy flow of talk," enlivened by aphorisms and epigrams, "pungent bits of absurdity." To talk pithily is necessarily to talk "pointedly and more or less audaciously"; but the exaggeration in such speech can be overlooked; even if it does border on the half-lie, it more than compensates by being one aspect of the truth seen in a startling way. The English would do well to slough off their mistaken conviction that brilliancy always hides shallowness and to emulate the French, whose language is "an instrument which makes even dull men talk and write like wits."

Such pleasures, however, can only be found in the city; and, indeed, Morley's tastes were urban. Although he did not share Macaulay's utter insensitiveness to country scenery, he nevertheless could agree with Samuel Johnson that when a man is tired of London he is tired of life. Rural landscape had its delights, to be sure, but occasional excursions into them sufficed; the contemplation of rural living made him writhe. He had no knowledge of gardening, and no taste for it; and he could not tolerate the prospect of being troubled by property repairs, pursued by carpenters and plumbers, pestered by moles and rats. In a village he would be conspicuous; his least movements would be the subject of every yokel's daily gossip. Worse still would be the inevitable young ladies, even more vapid in their flirtatious chatter than Belgravian belles—rustic damsels, most of them, who had never even so much as seen a leading article in a newspaper. Worst of all was the absence of any intellectual companionship, any stimulating conversation among men. In their stead were only the "Tyranny of Tattle" and the "Great God of Dulness," which were "ten times worse," he protested, than the expense and dirt and noise of London could ever be.

One last "adjunct of grace" remains. This one, however, is

hardly secondary; on the contrary, through the nurturing and preservation of it, Morley was immeasurably aided in giving his "existence an air of dignity and size and grandeur." It was a young man enriched and made eloquent by his relationships with Meredith and George Eliot and John Stuart Mill, who confided:

... it is in the consciousness of an occult sympathy that the charm and consolation of friendship resides, not in being a more privileged and more intimate kind of gossiper. In the most delicate kinds of friendship, a man or a woman, who thinks about it at all, cannot help feeling as Aladdin may have felt when, after accidentally rubbing the magician's ring, he first saw the genius of the ring appear, or when the genius of the lamp brought him delicious meats in golden vessels. There is an air of magic in the sudden perfection with which it is found that a whole set of new sympathies have sprung up, and a whole body of new pleasures been added to the old stock.

All his life he must be equal to the reciprocal respect and trust which high friendly affection entailed. He must retain his "flexibility and openness of spirit." The prime element in friendship, he believed, is always something like reverence, but without distance or abasement—a consciousness of "one's own partial inferiority"; a friend has some "grace of character that you have not."

"The fatal law," however, "that the side on which we are most susceptible of pleasure is also that on which we may have inflicted on us the greatest pain, applies as well to friendship as to all other occasions of emotion." All of us, victims of antithetical prejudices and antagonistic ideas, are prey to quarrels. Quarrels do occur—even with our best friends, and their occurrence must be accepted; only in that acceptance the fortunate efficacy of reconciliation must not be forgotten. What are inexcusable, and usually irremediable, are those half-deliberate quarrels that grow out of "gratuitous perversity" in human nature—out of caprice or jealousy. They are unmanly, and each of us must be on guard against them. All in all, given mutual appreciativeness and sincerity, friendships can be established and sustained, too, in spite of intellectual differences. Too many of us, unfortunately, in friendship as in morals, are in the habit of confusing right with duty. We must abstain from always speaking our minds and understand that "a certain willingness to hear opinions patiently and silently, in spite of a strong itch to controvert them, is absolutely necessary to keep the world from being a sheer bear garden."

III

Certainly the temper that provoked these reflections on life was far from optimistic. Indeed, acquaintance with it breeds the suspicion that it was one naturally inclined to pessimism—that Morley involuntarily saw bleakness and sensed hopelessness in human life but was buoyed up by his reason and his disciplined will and saved from sinking into the black pit.[4] Hostile to panaceas, incredulous of any "instantaneous and unimpeachable millennium," he knew that progress needed ceaseless human effort, that it was not an automaton with a capital letter. "The true faith in the future is, that things will move if they are made to move, and not unless." Whatsoever work his hand found to do, he did with all his might, and he agreed with Ecclesiastes in the advisability of the pursuit. But he would not go all the way with Ecclesiastes—or with a contemporary, Eugénie de Guérin either—in saying that it would have been better for man if he had not been born. He would not let himself despair. His resoluteness in facing life, however,

---

[4] In November, 1891, a discerning Frenchman, Augustin Filon, after a visit with him was to write in the *Revue des Deux Mondes* that he was innately melancholy: "From the first glance thrown about him, he had known that the world is evil, that it can become better, and that it will never be good; . . . One of the first in his time, one of the only ones among his race, in the midst of inane joviality or commercialized brutality, he has smelled the odor of death, that fine and delicate odor of autumnal dust that characterizes the ends of civilization and that some people, today, are savoring to the point of intoxication."

was not at all the same thing as a wishful self-deception. His eyes were open to all the uglinesses and tragic scars of existence; his achievement is that as a youth in the face of them he could shape the convictions which he did. "So long . . . as these . . . noxious elements [disease, bereavement, religious dilemma] are absent, a wise man, who does not expect more from life than the conditions of life can ever suffer it to give . . . who has with judgment fashioned out some predominant purpose, and at the same time kept all other sympathies and interests moderately accessible from without, has done as much as we mortals ever can to secure happiness of the best kind" and "will find within his reach a never-failing stock of adequate pleasures, which make his life very well worth living for." Thus Morley, turning his face to the future, determined to meet it with "a vigorous and stalwart stride," not "at best only a feeble hobbling."

Almost immediately he was confronted by the rising sun of a glorious day. Late in 1866, through the influence of G. H. Lewes and his Oxford friend, Cotter Morison, he was appointed to the editorship of *The Fortnightly Review*. His period of apprenticeship was over; though not yet twenty-eight, he had already become known among literary intellectuals. Here before him the horizon of a wide reputation was lighting up.

CHAPTER TWO

The Fortnightly Review (1867-1882)
Raising the Temperature of Thought through
Journalism

I

ACCORDING to Anthony Trollope, one of its initiators, *The Fortnightly Review* had been founded early in 1865 as a new periodical to be not only "good in its literature, but strictly impartial and absolutely honest." It was additionally distinguished by its inauguration of the policy of signature for all its articles, a policy inspired by the French system and so eccentric for its day in England that it led one Edinburgh publisher to believe the first editor's judgment impaired. When Morley took charge of *The Fortnightly*, however, it had fallen on lean days. Having cost its original investors the several thousands they had staked, it was now the property of its publishers, Chapman and Hall, and in spite of its name, appeared only once a month. Though Morley himself later explained that it did not have the same prestige or fulfill the same purpose as some of its more illustrious predecessors—*The Edinburgh* or *The Westminster*, for example—still, in his time it was in the front rank of journalistic shapers of public opinion, along with *The Cornhill* and *The Saturday Review*. And while it did not retain the complete eclecticism wished for it by its founders, it nevertheless carried the distinction in the 1870's of a challenging openness of mind on all controversial matters of religion, science, politics, and social reform; and the fifteen years (1867-1882) under Morley's supervision were perhaps the most influential of its whole existence, with an increasing circulation and distinguished contributors.

In his *Recollections* Morley defined its temper then as "rationalism without chill, in one sense, though with much of it in another." The tone of its leading articles was anything but cold; the effect of some of them on readers was chilling to the extreme. Huxley's famous essay, "On the Physical Basis of Life," for example, which came out in 1869, was almost as sensational in its way as Burke's *Reflections on the French Revolution* had been earlier and froze the last few theological arguments of doubters shivering in the struggle between religion and science.

What, in detail, the circumstances were, surrounding Morley's appointment to the editorship of *The Fortnightly*, is not known. In his own words it was Cotter Morison, the brilliant and versatile older friend responsible for his exposure at Oxford to Carlyle and Emerson, through whose influence he obtained the position. On request, he appeared for an interview one day before Trollope, only to be almost blown down by a sudden blast from the novelist who leaped from his seat behind his desk, "glaring as if in fury through his spectacles, and roaring like a bull of Bashan . . . 'Now, do you believe in the divinity of our beloved Lord and Savior Jesus Christ?' "

But, whether or not he was satisfied with the answer, the truth is that Trollope made a wise selection when he hired Morley, for he possessed superlative qualifications for such an office. At the outset he was distinguished by his ardent interest in all that was passing in the world. Although he never attempted a Baconian embracing of all knowledge for his province, it is likely that few journalists in London could have matched his fund of information about history, philosophy, science, politics, literature, and art. Furthermore, no one his age could have laid more valid claim to the very quality he had early placed a premium on—intellectual intrepidity, already exemplified in his style by an unusual gift for telling phrases. Not for nothing had he grown up in the factory streets of

Blackburn, where people were accustomed "even in the repose of ordinary intercourse to a naked vehemence of style that might seem to an innocent stranger to signal the near breakup of society" and where they gave and took "as pleasant banter, such crude pungencies as in other places would be wiped out in blood." Not for nothing either had he been bred on the Bible, impressing his ear with the sonority of its diction and his imagination with the grandeur of its figures. And not for nothing had he become steeped in science, as he showed in *Studies in Conduct* when he condemned contemporary style for having "no backbone in it"; "leaving the order of vertebrates," he complained, "it has sunk down to lower classes, among mere molluscs and jelly fish and other flabby organizations." Aware of the trenchant, tireless power of his own mind, he had decided: "It is not the assiduous cultivation of a style as such, but the cultivation of the intellect and feelings which produces good writing. Style comes of brooding over ideas, not words."

But beyond his endowments of a wide curiosity and a strenuous, fearless mind, he was set apart from other men by two further distinctions: an extraordinary mental training, imparted by Mill, and a wide historical perspective, derived from readings in Comte. There is no doubt that contact with Mill tooled and sharpened Morley's mind, gave speed, incisiveness, and accuracy to it until it was dexterous and piercing, not infallible in the conclusions it reached, but unerring in its stroke. His skill as a critical analyst was greatly developed by the older man. It was Mill's own ability to strip an argument, to peel back layer after layer of the integument and penetrate to the core, to which he approximated. If Mill was the Saint of Rationalism, Morley became its militant crusader.

The ideas of Auguste Comte were first revealed to Morley by Cotter Morison at Oxford, but he underwent no indoctrination until later in his London apprenticeship when he became intimate with Frederic Harrison, George Eliot, and G. H. Lewes, all devotees of Comte, in whose company he met Richard Congreve, the chief English apostle. As late as 1871 his thinking was so imbued with Comtian principle that he acknowledged to his friend Harrison, "That my whole idea of history is his is certain; that my particular ideas in nearly all the subordinate points are his, is not less certain."

Comte had seen that history was an evolution through successive stages of civilization from simple, primitive societies to those more complex and enlightened. His Positivism declared all historical periods to be interrelated through cause and effect, and all historical events to be phenomena understandable only through a knowledge of the conditions in which they occurred. The positive attitude, in short, was the scientific attitude, and was founded on a number of laws, chief among them the Law of the Three States, for Morley "the most important law at which the science of history" had yet arrived, which decreed that every piece of knowledge had passed, or must pass, through three states of growth, the theological, the metaphysical, and the positive. Every kind of belief, fetichism in religion, for example, was referable to a certain stage of development of the minds of the men who adhered to it, and was never to be criticized as a thing apart from the social conditions in which it flourished. Because it had fulfilled certain definite needs for human beings at a time, it was explainable only by an understanding of those needs.

Influenced by Positivism, Morley arrived at a definition of the "historic conception" as "a reference of every state of society to a particular stage in the evolution of its general conditions." This he employed as a measuring rod in estimating greater literary figures than himself—Voltaire among others—more than once to find them wanting under the application of it. It was the most valuable element of the Comtist philosophy which he acquired.

Another, for a time no less dear, was Comte's Religion of

Humanity, which to many sensitive men disillusioned by science seemed a solacing substitute for Christianity. A vital spiritual longing in Morley himself, for a time frustrated by his break from the church, was satisfied when Comte showed humanity to deserve the same devotion and service which the Christian deity had hitherto received. He was reassured in writing *Voltaire* that "that swelling consciousness of height and freedom with which the old legends of an omnipotent divine majesty fill the breast, may still remain; for how shall the universe ever cease to be a sovereign wonder of overwhelming power and superhuman fixedness of law?"

Comte's scheme for including in Humanity's Pantheon all those who had contributed notably to the march of civilization also found favor with him. It assisted the growth of his historical broadmindedness and in part accounted for his undertaking later enthusiastic studies of men so mutually antagonistic as De Maistre and Condorcet, Rousseau and Voltaire, Cromwell and Burke. That he could interest himself in the separate members of these pairs almost simultaneously has seemed unintelligible to some observers of his career. But he pointed out that, while the philosophies of two great figures of the same age might have nothing at all in common, each of them could contain elements which, taken individually, would be beneficial to the human race. And he gave additional support to his stand by citing one of his favorite assimilated dicta on such matters—Voltaire's words to Condorcet: "It is the part of a man like you to have preferences but no exclusions."

Equipped as he was with his intellectual advantages, it was Morley's task as editor, first, to enlist noteworthy contributors to *The Fortnightly* and, second, to act in relation to them as a director or guide—to impart through his own writing some general character or tone to the *Review*. In his obtaining of contributors he was extraordinarily successful. Nobody who takes the time today to read through even a volume of his *Fort-*

nightly can repress sighs of admiration over the diversity and significance of the subjects he encounters, or the consistent brilliance with which they are illuminated. The foremost writers in England all took part—Arnold, Swinburne, Meredith, Rossetti, Bagehot, Huxley, Pater, Lewes, Harrison, Dicey, Stephen, Pattison, and Myers. In the leadership which he demonstrated with his own work, Morley was zealous and indefatigable. Although he never strove to stamp an actual policy on his periodical, he did transmit, through his reviews and pieces written in an editorial capacity, as well as through his special, independent, longer contributions, the tenets of the Liberalism he had learned from John Stuart Mill. "Respect for the dignity and worth of the individual," he stated afterwards was its root. It stood "for pursuit of social good against class interest or dynastic interest . . . for the subjection to human judgment of all claims of external authority, whether in an organized church, or in more loosely gathered societies of believers, or in books held sacred." In law-making it attended first to "the higher characteristics of human nature," and in executive administration, it counted on mercy "as a wise supplement to terror." It was the opposite of militarism and it was rooted in a belief in progress.

Indeed much progress had already been made, yet the ground still to be covered was vast. To be sure, slavery and the slave trade had been abolished, strict conformity to the Thirty-nine Articles as a condition for entrance at the universities had been removed, the bars against Catholics in public office had been lifted, the Corn Laws had been exchanged for a more rational and more humane system of tariffs, and the voting franchise had been extended and improvements in municipal government effected; but Morley was alive to the fact that only recently had the last vestige of slavery in the new world disappeared and that the first Catholic undergraduate in Lincoln College at Oxford had been there in his own time. The franchise must be spread even further; a reputable system of state-supported education must be developed; the living conditions of working people must be made sanitary, and wage-and-hour laws passed; the church must be made a free and separate institution from the state; and women must be recognized as participating members of an active society and be educated for social responsibility.

From Mill's examination of the whole matter of liberty, Morley had learned the responsibility which the state must assume for the members of society, but he had discovered as well that the state has no right to interfere with the activity of any individual unless it has begun to injure the well-being or impede the freedom of movement of another. He had been inspired by the unselfishness and dignity in Mill's conception of the useful, intelligent member of society, whose inviolable right to freedom of belief, speech, and action finds its noblest employment in causes beneficial to the greatest number of his fellow men. Such a conception puts a premium on intelligence as well as on a refined ethical sense, but Mill, saintly himself, had confidence in human beings—or rather in the rationality of a number of them large and influential enough to supply the motive power in social growth. And it was his trust in the power of a community of educated, thinking men and women which Morley derived. Finally, from frequent contact with such ideas as saw light in print in the famous "On the Subjection of Women," Morley came to be clear-headed about female intelligence and to champion its right to equal development with that of men. Progress, then, through enlightenment. And the Liberal way, with its Utilitarian admixture, was the enlightened way.

Although Morley had forsworn an ecclesiastical pulpit in his later days at Oxford, the zeal of the preacher and the reformer had not died in him by 1867; *The Fortnightly* would become his pulpit and he would inveigh from it. His correspondence with Frederic Harrison shows that he himself recognized the different character of the pulpit he had attained; and Harrison, amused by the transfer of allegiance, playfully summed him up "as an apostle or rather entrepreneur of apostles. Let us say for short Diderot plus John Wesley." So convinced was he, however, of the necessity of the message he was to transmit and so sure of its indispensability to the salvation of England, that his fervency led him often into excesses of statement which came dangerously close to claiming infallibility. Since the least of his words would be a *fiat*, he was moved now and then to write them all large. Even in his earliest essays for *The Saturday Review* there had been flashes of overstatement; moved by his scorn of cant, his impetuousness, he had more than once dismissed arguments with a single fact or two in refutation and then the hyperbolic remark that with "a hundred other cases" or "in a thousand other ways" or by "ten thousand other things" he could adduce additional proof.

This impatience and this urge to be high-handed were sometimes mitigated, however, by his realization of the weightiness of his editorship. In his less heated moments, when he reflected that his was part of the "immeasurably momentous task of forming national opinion," the consciousness of his association with *The Fortnightly* had "a very strong and perceptible influence" upon him, and he strove to restrain the deep desire "to erect himself Pope and Sir Oracle," which "lies in the spirit of a man with strong convictions." Continual restraint, however, was too difficult. His tone was the tone of the apostle militant; it even at times rang with something of gladiatorial pugnacity. In the first year of his leadership he wrote a brief but challenging manifesto in which he sounded the call to arms in behalf of the new journalism of signature. Having already seen signs that England was "on the eve of an era of free speech" and without taking the pains to list more than "one or two of the hundred symptoms" of it, he incited all the journalistic die-hards for anonymity and all men of his "own way of thinking" to fight it out—"with no button at the ends" of their foils. Irrepressibly proud that hostilities had already begun, he welcomed more signing of articles not alone for increased honesty and clarity but so that there could be "more hard hitting."

It was not only the consciousness of his position, however, which prompted Morley to polemical excesses. Much of his barbed derision in *The Fortnightly's* pages, much of what is indistinguishable from out-and-out truculence, can be accounted for by the delight he took as a combatant in the flawless functioning of the weapon with which he was fighting—his acute, untiring mind. Emboldened by his intellectual vigor and intrepidity, he often strode beyond the limits of good taste. How else can one explain his occasional lapses into the two qualities of debate which he had earlier abjured—vindictiveness and vilification? The best way of observing the vigor of his mind, as well as the subjects toward which it was directed, is in retracing exactly what he spent fifteen years in laying down and marking clearly, "the line of passage from sentimental Radicalism to scientific Liberalism." As he drew it, the route was distinguished by its penetration of certain areas of contested ground.

II

First among these regions of dispute was religion. Morley considered it almost an English instinct to feel strongly about this subject; even indifferentism, he had observed, had a constant tendency among Englishmen "to become venomous and acrid." And indeed his own behavior offered no exception to the rule. He bore an unyielding hostility to theology because its dogma outraged his reason. In what were for him the Eternal Verities, he was a ruthless rationalist. Before he had reached his majority he had taken the trouble to ascertain whether his religion was supernatural or not, and so from *The Fortnightly's* pages he openly charged anyone who had not taken the same pains with "either cowardice or the most ignoble kind of indolence." Holding with Socrates and Mill that good conduct was inseparable from enlightened conduct, he lashed out at the current notion that "truths external to the mind" could be known by intuition or revelation because he was "persuaded" that it was for his times the chief "intellectual support of false doctrines and bad institutions." Nor did he have any patience with pseudo-rationalists who pursued the most exacting Biblical scholarship and laid claim to religious enlightenment, when in reality they were only substituting a tracing of "the history of a conception or group of conceptions, for a scientific inquiry into its truth and its correspondence with reality or fitness." They might be able to discourse fluently on the metaphysical subtleties of the Church Fathers, but they had shirked the responsibility of deciding whether traditional Christian theology answered the questions raised by nineteenth-century industrial civilization. Theirs was a "vicious habit," and the widespread practicing of it contributed powerfully to the continuation of the lamentable "religious anarchy" in England.

Fundamental in the Christian scheme of things, it was the postulation of an omniscient, omnipotent, benevolent Deity which Morley could not stomach. Any theodicy which exhorted its adherents to believe that a supreme Being was personally interested in the welfare of each one of them when all about there raged needless, undeserved pain, suffering, disease, and waste, was anathema. The farther one's eye travelled, the wider his horizon became, the more evident it became that much of what people called Nature—God's handiwork—was only a "vast torment of blind and viewless forces." Without purpose, the world was equally without an underlying moral law. What evidence of divine retribution could be discerned on a globe where, from time immemorial, the beings who attained highest earthly power and greatest reputation were only the most ruth-

less and accomplished slaughterers of their fellows? In deadly
earnest and steeled to draw blood in the encounter with all
cowards who tricked their understandings and played "fast
and loose with words," Morley execrated the "omnipotent Being for whose diversion the dismal panorama of all the evil
work done under the sun was bidden to unfold itself" and who
saw that it was very good; while the garment of natural theology for "covering the phenomena of existence," he kicked
into the gutter for a "sorry rag."

The church, as an institution protecting, preserving, and
disseminating such a theodicy had seen its day; it was doomed
and must go. Not that it had made no contribution to mankind.
On the contrary, Morley was keenly alive to its great work in
the past. In what he held were wrongly called the Dark Ages,
the mediaeval church, in spite of "many imperfections and
some crimes," had done what no achievement of physical science could hope to vie with: it had purified men's appetites, set
"discipline and direction on their lives," and offered to the
world "new types of moral obligation and fairer ideals of
saintly living," whose light even in 1875 still radiated like a
beacon to guide the "poor voyages" of human beings. Nevertheless, the church, in spite of its ethical illumination and inspiration through the centuries, must be made to stand henceforth on
its own foundations. In England in the nineteenth century,
science demanded that it be disestablished and separated from
the state, obliged to support itself on funds raised by itself. So,
too, because of the falseness of its theology, its hand must be
removed from any further connection with education in England; the taint of its doctrines in children's minds was a menace
to the intellectual welfare of the nation no longer tolerable.

Morley's fervidness as a leader in the campaign for disestablishment led him to use the slightest editorial circumstance as
an occasion for venting his wrath. His militant antipathy in-
serted itself somewhere into almost every piece he wrote for

The Fortnightly—into the briefest review of a book of travels as well as into what might otherwise have been a perfunctory series of remarks on an approaching election. He was too indignant, too impatient to allow men to be gradually disabused of their religious error. "Silent dissolution," though it might well be "the most pacific process" of enlightening mankind, was objectionable because it entailed a long intermediate period "of confused and debilitating half-belief." The sudden, direct shock of disillusionment was preferable, because in the long run, it would be seen to have braced and invigorated "the understanding." In his excessive eagerness, however, to accelerate the dissolution, he became almost nihilistic. Now he sneered at the "cant of timorous theologians"; now he laughed at the "screams of infuriated theological auxiliaries" of the benighted landed gentry as they cowered before the handwriting on the wall; now he shouted for the exposure of "that sinister clerical army of twenty-eight thousand men in masks." But it was in an inoffensive-looking article entitled "The Political Prelude" that he poured the full measure of his anger and contempt on the heads of the representatives of a church quick to ratify national arrogance but unable to afford the thinnest shred of national moral guidance. In his vilifying vocabulary, clergymen emerged as intellectual eunuchs—robbed of their cerebral energies by the bishops who had laid hands on their heads, rendering them creatures of immutable "mental sterility" in a ceremony not wholly unlike the Oriental way of producing "incomparable guardians of the seraglio." They existed as ecclesiastical tools for whom declining to use their minds to the best of their capacity was "held laudable and excellent"— as parasites who flourished by fastening themselves on three great branches of society: on women, who through a lack of intellectual cultivation, would "easily imbibe violent religious prejudices"; on "that immense mass of disinterested stupidity ["a great hive of Troglodytes"] which exists in all countries";

and on the "anti-social classes, the great landowners, and the squires," whose own time of reckoning was not far distant.

Besides attacking the outgrown conventional religion, however, Morley was alert in defending the new and modern religion which he and others equally enlightened had embraced— the non-theological religion in which love of humanity and zeal to work for it, to assist in the movement of progress, in short, had taken the place of primary motivation formerly occupied by the injunctions of a supernatural deity. It was like Christianity only in that Christ's system of ethics was retained. When the new faith was charged with being bleak, with having nothing like the "beauties of association" of traditional Christianity with which to stir human imagination, he was forced to admit that there was something chilling about its starkness. But after all, he countered, was not Christianity itself in the days of its origin bare likewise and dismissed by fashionable, cosmopolitan followers of "mellowed pagan philosophy as crude, meagre, jejune, dreary"? Was it not likely, then, that the new faith, through the centuries to come, would enrich itself and take on attractive warmth and coloring?

When Morley used the words "science" and "scientific," he was not thinking of any particular branch of knowledge like chemistry or physics or zoology, though he was well informed on almost all such branches; he had in mind a way of thinking, of looking at life, according to which all the phenomena of existence—biological, psychological, religious, aesthetic, social, or political—were products of natural forces that could be studied and measured. Because Comte had stressed the interrelatedness of all phenomena and the continuity of history, he was the adopted leader of the scientific intellectuals in England in the 'sixties and 'seventies. And he lent impetus to their belief in progress, too, for the growth he had discovered, in mental conceptions as well as in forms of society, was invariably upward, in the direction of something better and more civilized. Just as philosophical monotheism was superior to fetichism as an explanation of life, so positivism was superior to monotheism. Thus, if there was growth, there was progress, and it was an invincible belief in progress that was cemented as the cornerstone of the faith for the future.

As *The Fortnightly's* preacher, Morley showed how our gratitude to the thinkers and workers of the past for the benefits they have bequeathed us ought to stimulate us to play some part, no matter how small, in the transmission of still greater benefits for the generations to come. Eventually, there will be a millennium, in which all human aspirations for the betterment of earthly living will be consummated. To be sure, since he had protested earlier, in *The Saturday Review*, against "short cuts" and "an instantaneous and unimpeachable" millennium, he did not predict finality of achievement in the following century. After all, progress was not steadily continuous and automatic. Its law was like the "law" by which a locomotive ran on rails leading eventually to a fixed and single terminus. Consider, he asked, what happened to that "law" when "a malignant or incompetent or careless driver" got behind the throttle; imagine the derailment, the rooting up of the earth, the destruction of human life, the obstructing of the way. Yet in spite of the fact that progress was "a tardy, stumbling, blind, and most extravagantly wasteful process," the millennium would come if men worked for it, countless ages in the future though it might be.

Striving as one of those self-dedicated to insuring the advent of the millennium, Morley was unshakable in his conviction that the last page in the book of progress had been unturned, that the depths of human capacity remained not only untapped but unsighted. When doubters confronted him with the question whether a democratic organization was not incompatible with social advance, whether, for instance, there were not greater strides forward in a society solidified by strict unity of belief, he answered with a stout denial. Consider, he urged, the Byzantine Empire or any of "the great theocracies, ancient Egypt, Islam under the Caliphs, India under the Buddhists or Brahmins." And when sterile hangers-on, fearful that the incrustations over their minds would be scraped, protested against his desire to destroy decaying ideas, he reminded them that progress was not entirely a negativing movement, for there could be seen occurring a "growth of notions newer and more enduring." Real leaders in the cause of progress were builders, who, like Descartes, did not just "pull down the existing edifice of crumbling convictions and tottering traditions, and then leave men naked and houseless." After demolishing the old, they "laid the more stable foundations of the new."

The science of history, as Morley spoke of it, was simply another name for the dynamic branch of the science of sociology; it could be called, in short, "social dynamics," and the only really valid system of it owed its origin to Comte. Social dynamics sought an embracing knowledge of the whole of a past culture—all its beliefs, its domestic customs, its arts, its commercial, political, and industrial systems; and once it had amassed data about a number of cultural groups, it set out to trace the relations between them, to follow the "succession and order" in which they evolved, interpreting connections always in strict terms of cause and effect. In the light of such a taxing procedure, "history, properly so-called," appeared as nothing more than "descriptive sociology," providing raw material for the larger, more general study, for it was not concerned with discovering the laws that governed "the entire evolution," but explored "only a part of the succession of historical events," and sought "not the ultimate but the proximate causes of the facts of modern" civilizations.

Not all people, of course, shared such opinions. Eminent writers challenged the assumption that any study of the past, no matter how prolonged and brain-consuming, could be scientific. How could any occurrence three thousand years old be judged in terms of cause and effect? Among Morley's antagonists was James Anthony Froude, who maintained that since a historian, to be scientific, would have to limit himself to influences which were "palpable and ponderable" and necessarily neglect all the unmeasurable thoughts and affections and emotions of men, he would be giving a sorry, shrunken picture of historical development. Morley, however, retaliated with the assertion that imponderables, no less than ponderables, were fit subjects for the scientific historian's research; "the intense convictions of men" were "at least as much the property of history as their outward actions." When Froude asked with finality, "Will a time ever be when the lost secret of the foundation of Rome can be recovered by historic laws? If not, where is our science of history?" he was answered by mocking analogy: "This is exactly as if somebody were to say, 'Will a time ever be when meteorological laws can tell us whether it was a wet or a fine day at Jericho a thousand years ago? If not, where is our science of meteorology?' " And when he cited free will as a separate, autonomous agency inside man making it impossible to record his behavior in terms of cause and effect, he was accused out-and-out of "abject fatalism." To think of the will as an independent instrument, miraculously given and made to function in the flux of circumstance in varying, unpredictable directions, exclusive of antecedents, is to make man "the victim and sport of a supernatural force." It is much more reasonable to call a human being free "when you believe his will to follow determinate antecedents—desires, aversions, habits of character, opportunity—because antecedents are controllable." By so believing, it is possible early in life to take pains to make one's "virtuous desires and aversions predominant." This, announced Morley, is the scientific, as opposed to the theological, view of human character.

Froude further represented the undesirable theological outlook on history in his assertion that there is a moral order in
the universe discernible in the system of retribution which is
part of the nature of things. Morley dismissed such an asseveration with contempt. The only retribution which scientific investigation exposes can be contained in the law, "he that is unjust,
let him be unjust still, and he which is filthy, let him be filthy
still." If there is no moral order, however, there is scientific
order. Conditions produce results invariably, and man as a
rational animal can be shown to have learned gradually how
to escape inimical effects by avoiding their causes. History,
then, apart from justice and moral right and wrong, is not a
"chaotic agglomeration of intricate accidents" but an "intelligible array of orderly sequences."

All of this is not to say, however, that morality has played no
part in history and is not a potent force in the active life of a
nation. With the distinction always in his mind between what
a man knows to be right and his will or desire to practice it,
Morley admitted that "The immediate cause of the decline of a
people is nearly always a decline in the quantity of its conscience, not a depravation of its theoretical ethics," and he
cited as evidences of this fact the ancient Greek decay, as well
as the Christian fall before the Saracens at Constantinople and
in Spain. Quantity of conscience, to pursue the analysis further, is derived from intellectual vigor and cannot exist apart
from it; it is always the legal code which grows first and the
ethical code which "follows steadily behind it," so that although
"moral dogmas" do advance, they do so only by the impetus
they derive from "intellectual processes." Thus the "great
moral reformer" can be defined as "simply the man who brings
the healthiest and strongest intellect into questions of conduct
and character, instead of into chemistry, physiology, or any
other science." And in any civilization, therefore, "the high
moral type" is not that which conforms to a divine system of

ethics, received intuitively, but "that which best meets the requirements of the situation, and it flows from the very definition that the low moral type will fall before it, and be visited by ruin."

Just as the force of morality (quantity of conscience) had played a measurable part in history, so the study of history itself possessed a recognizable moral value and was an instrument of "practical moral significance." Through a deepening of perspective, it was the best means of awakening a child to a consciousness of his debt to the past and of fostering in him the desirable feelings of gratitude, humility, and solicitude for the future. That one was scientific in his study of history did not mean that he had to remain absolutely impartial in the face of facts revealed, that he had to forego the privilege (for Morley, the necessity) of making up his mind about things. Science should develop and sharpen discrimination, not nullify it. No one was obliged to consider the deeds of Aurelian and Napoleon with the same dispassionate scrutiny with which he would watch the oxidation of sulphur or the emergence of a butterfly from its chrysalis. Now it was history seen thus, as an invaluable means of nurturing the highest moral consciousness, which made Morley assign it to a fundamental place in his plan for reform of a subject with which he as a Liberal leader was all his life passionately concerned—education.

Of all the pages which he wrote as the official polemist of *The Fortnightly*, none were more timely, more controversial, or more effectual than those which composed *The Struggle for National Education*. He was fighting for a complete reform of the English elementary school system, and since at bottom the weakness and the evil of that system lay in a state-promoted association of school instruction with the established church, he found, in his ecclesiastical antipathy, a ready-to-hand incitement to strong language and incontrovertible argument. It was in this polemic that he struck off his most succinct, and yet most comprehensive, condemnation of the record of the church in England, which, he said, in "every other great crisis" except that of 1688 had "made herself the ally of tyranny, the organ of social oppression, the champion of intellectual bondage." But apart from such vituperation of the church and her clergy, expert always at dressing up "obscurantism in preacher's phrases and Bible precedents," he showed how slightly more than a fourth of all the children in England over six emerged from their school training without being able to read the Bible, write the slightest letter coherently, or do any more in arithmetic than add six and four. It was not only that most of the training of teachers was controlled by the church or that too much of the actual instruction of the children was of a religious cast; it was that the quality of the teaching was so bad everywhere that even the church catechism in wholly sectarian schools was scrappily learned and disgracefully misunderstood. What must be established was a complete system of state-supported schools, in which instruction would be entirely secular. It was imperative for the government to accept the education of young people as "one of the highest of national duties" instead of neglecting it as "a superfluity left to the sects."[1] What a deplorable example England offered in requiring her children to pass only five years of their lives in school (from eight to thirteen) and in subjecting them to the haphazard tutelage of teachers who were not university-bred and were abysmally deficient in mathematics, grammar, geography, and history! How she suffered

---

[1] In writing on social responsibilities for *Macmillan's* back in 1866, Morley, already fond of taunting those to whom government centralization was a "bugbear," had condemned England's inveterate "sluggishness" over reform and looked with admiration on the colony of Victoria; there denominational differences were not barriers to nationalization and "the preposterous right" was denied to parents "of pleasing themselves whether their children" should "grow up in darkness or enlightenment." He did not, however, advocate excluding ministers from membership on English school boards; "Disqualification never made anybody better." A clergyman-trustee having to co-operate with laymen as his equals could not but become enlightened.

by comparison with the United States, where, Morley had learned firsthand from "a professor at a university in one of the great towns of the West," young men and women were equipped to go directly from elementary school to college, deeply enough imbued with the desire for higher learning that some, to earn their way, "would rise at four or five in the morning to make their day's bread by distributing the morning papers," while others would "light the lamps in the streets," and still others would go "down to the town every afternoon to earn a dinner by shaving at a barber's"!

Cynics and habitual do-nothings deprecated Morley's rudeness in the attack he was leading. What if his plans for educational reform were all adopted? There would be no millennium. But such a protest was no deterrent. A millennium it might not be, but what a "substantial social gain"! It is true, he conceded, that the soundest of elementary trainings will not make people virtuous or moral, or inflexibly good citizens, but it will give them a better chance to become so. At the very least, they will be enabled to take care of their own affairs. The time has passed when "rude vigour" could be complacently trusted "as a substitute for trained intelligence." Better education is imperative now that "ignorant multitudes" are the "political masters of the realm."

Just what this better education should be, once the machinery for dispensing it had been perfected, Morley knew thoroughly. In an address on popular culture delivered in Town Hall, Birmingham, on October 5, 1876, to open that year's session of the Midland Institute, he gave a clear exposition of his plan. He desired to see eventually a national state of affairs in which a young man could be "educated at a day-school in his own town," have the opportunity of following higher education there, and be taught "at the earliest convenient time . . . to earn his own living." The popular education to which he would be exposed should aim to develop in him "the habit of valuing, not merely speculative or scientific truth, but the truth of practical life," for it was the "intellectual conscience" in people that needed growth, and the greatest advance which could be imagined was one in which all men—and particularly all women—would have learned "to quantify their propositions."

In its diffusing of knowledge, popular education should rid itself of what had all along been its repellent harshness, its offensive vein of ascetic and puritanical rigorousness. After all, looked at humanly, one of the chief aims of modern schools ought to be to teach people how to amuse and refresh themselves "in a rational rather than an irrational manner"; and so, in their reading of literature, for instance, students should be given the key to the most stimulating and pleasurable set of books in the world, those in the French language. It was because French, in addition to its "clearness, firmness, and order," was distinguished by something not possessed by English —"liveliness in union with urbanity"—that more men and women in England would profit by learning it.

The curriculum which Morley recommended was general; yet he took every precaution to prevent his listeners from confusing "general" with "superficial." Having a general knowledge did mean knowing only general truths, but it meant knowing them thoroughly and in relation to one another and was not at all incompatible with being methodical. And just as it was better to read, in place of Racine's plays, the essays of Sainte-Beuve because they bore a closer relation to contemporary life, so it was more valuable to digest and correlate the significant facts, the leading ideas, in such subjects as logic, mathematics, geometry, chemistry, astronomy, and natural history instead of laboring year in and year out over the exacting details of Latin grammar, the metrical intricacies of Latin poetry, or the perplexing subtleties of theological dogma. What was essential was that the mind of the student be acclimated to the intellectual atmosphere of his own age, that he understand himself socially as well as biologically in the complex civilization of the nineteenth century. And since, as Morley never tired of repeating, there was no better way of understanding the present and one's relation to it than through an intelligent study of the past, the most valuable subject in any system of popular education was history—not taught as a series of dates and kingships, beginning arbitrarily with England in 901 or 1066 or 1603 or 1688, but as an enlightening vision of the growth of the western world. Through a survey from Greek civilization through Roman culture, Mohammedan culture, and medieval Christian society, to the development of modern Europe during the Renaissance, students could be made to see the linking of centuries —in short, the oneness of history, its greatest fact. The broad, continuous lines of the development of occidental civilization would be imprinted on their minds. This would be its immeasurable intellectual advantage. But there was an additional profit, a moral one. History so studied, with people learning to see both the beginning and the end of things, "to look before and after" as well as at, would result in an enrichment of character, always "a higher thing than mere intellect"; it would tend to make human personality "constantly alive with the spirit of beneficence." The complaint that "the commonest people" would not grasp or respond to such a course, Morley rejected summarily. "How do we know"? he asked; "We have never yet . . . tried the height and pitch to which our people are capable of rising."

Separate from popular education was what Morley called academic education, the product of universities, whose function was not only to diffuse the body of existing knowledge but to increase it. Ever since his Oxford days, however, he had known that this object was abused, even at England's highest institutions, by an almost universal preoccupation with crew-racing and rugby and cricket and the planning of social delights for the holiday. Nevertheless, in spite of prevalent distractions the

attempt ought not to be abandoned to demonstrate to young men
that a university, in fulfilling its function of increasing knowledge, must turn out individuals conspicuous, first, for "intellectual strenuousness," and second, for a deep love of ideas and
"unswerving devotion to truth." With the increasing strife between science and the classics over a place of supremacy in an
academic curriculum to achieve such an end, Morley had no
patience. The antagonism was "fruitless and senseless"; both
science and classical literature supplied far too special and
valuable materials "to the modern intellect" for either to be
dispensed with. Equally needed, neither could be called "the
best educational instrument."

Because he believed so firmly that women, even more than
men, would benefit by learning how to "quantify their propositions," Morley gave considerable time and thought during his
Fortnightly incumbency to the support of movements for female
betterment. An interesting evidence of his strong-rooted convictions on the subject is his unhesitating, and surprising, declaration that Mill's essay "On the Subjection of Women" was more
important than his searching "On Liberty." The essay on liberty was an exposition in the abstract, whereas that on the
subordination of women was a concrete application; its "accurate and unanswerable reasoning," its "noble elevation," its
"sagacity" of "maxims on conduct and character," the "beauty
of its aspirations for the improvement of collective social life"
—all these made it more significant and more consequential.
But although he continued, in reviews and editorials, to maintain that women needed more education and a more active
public life as a necessary stimulus to both their intellectual and
emotional faculties, there is nothing in *The Fortnightly* con-
struable as a feminist policy on his part. On at least one occasion he even took issue with women over what constituted a
government act beneficial to their own sex. In "A Short Letter

to Some Ladies," he demonstrated vigorously his modernness
of mind of which he was so proud, his steadfastness in looking
the most objectionable of facts in the face. When asked to join
the Ladies' Association for the Repeal of the Contagious Dis-
eases Acts, acts by which the government sought to check the
spread of syphilis through the medical inspection and treatment
of prostitutes, he had flatly refused. The ladies, in their aversion to the government's practice, were undoubtedly well-mean-
ing, but they were sentimental. Why must people imagine that
every human being, no matter how rotten or demoralized, still
possessed an infinite capacity for self-improvement and would
respond promptly and eagerly to the slightest benevolence?
Prostitution was a fact; not only that, for his generation it was
so rampant and rooted that it was "practically . . . as if it were
a necessity." As for its origin, there was "no more effective
cause of the misconduct of vicious women" in England, the
indignant ladies were informed, "than the misconduct of virtuous ones." Young girls, when employed as servants or seam-
stresses by the most respectable families, were usually shockingly underpaid and treated with an intolerable coldness or
"inhuman reserve." Under such circumstances, they were
driven to the streets. And in the long run it was not "much
more degrading and soul-destroying and fundamentally immoral to wear away a life in pandering to the coarse appetite
of one sex than in pandering to the ignoble and monstrous
vanity of the other."

When, in January 1873, Morley wrote an editorial protesting heatedly against the "atrocious wrong" committed by certain moneyed London newspapers and a prejudiced judge in
subjecting five gas stokers guilty of conspiring to break a
"Masters and Servants Act," to a sentence four times harsher
than it should have been according to the law by which alone
they ought to have been tried, he was not voicing a new-born

concern for working men. Next to religion and along with politics, the theme of labor was of longest standing with him. In the early 1860's already implanted in his mind was the question: would the increase in national wealth make for more equal distribution or not? That was the most important thing to consider about the new order. In 1866 he was berating the English for the impotence of what they called their public opinion, for although there was widespread knowledge of the barbarous conditions among child-laborers, it was knowledge accompanied by no feeling and so unable to institute any reform. Social apathy in the face of increasingly rapid industrial advance was throwing into gloomier and gloomier light the future of those who toiled; the workers' problem had become "the great proletarian tragedy." Again and again in *The Fortnightly* he lamented the "profuse and ruthless using up of human life merely in the way of business." Unremittingly he called attention to the movement for the emancipation of the industrial classes as the distinguishing movement of the century; it was an advantage "for all the highest interests of society," alongside which everything else, "even convulsions of faith," had to be subordinate. And what a theme for the future historian—as inspiring as it was grand and inescapable! After all, was not the rise of the masses to a preponderance in political control a rise unaccompanied by any partisan or factional motives, for the reason that the masses constituted no class at all but were the body of the people? "The claims of the multitude are sovereign and paramount, exactly because it is the multitude."

In his own lifetime Morley had seen an almost magical transformation of the material lot of workers. In his childhood men were imprisoned for combining to ask for higher wages, and the brutalizing squalor in which their families were condemned to live allowed illiteracy, immorality, and disease to menace them constantly. Factory men, rotting under the curse of liquor, carried their drink along with them into the works, and in the towns there was dog fighting every Saturday afternoon. But by the end of the second year of his editorship the picture had been improved. The right of laborers to combine and form unions had been insured through their vigorous defence and championship by his own friend, Frederic Harrison. Already in Lancashire towns thousands of factory families were benefiting from co-operative stores and mills; and their houses, unimaginative, but solid and well painted, were to be seen lining the streets of the towns, neat, clean, and regular. The core of the population was thrifty, healthy, stable, self-respecting, not to be matched even in the United States for its capacity to use advantageously its abundance of insurpassable means to "decent and happy living." True, many mothers of families still worked in the mills all day, but their industrious labor left them better off than if they had dawdled at home. And although much drunkenness still remained to be combatted and some two thousand villages in England had not yet been roused from their political torpor, the movement for industrial reform, it must be remembered, had only just begun. On the whole, Morley was convinced that the best type of mill worker was as good as the best representatives of "active humanity" anywhere else, and the best type abounded.

The recurrence of strikes was as regrettable and as much a cause of concern to Morley as to any other social-minded man of his time. Strife between employer and employe pained him; and he knew that it was most deplorable, not for the material damage or physical injury which it strewed, but for its psychological consequences, the seeds of increased suspicion and resentment which it sowed in the minds of the mill owner and his paid hands, aggravating the original source of antagonism, and rendering more unlikely the chances for a reasonable, equitable reconciliation. What could be done about such dissension? Of some things, he was certain. Strikes would never be

obviated, just as he had years ago discovered that quarrels
between friends cannot be wished away. Human beings are
human, and wherever they are, the possibility of discord exists.
But that is not to say that the number of strikes cannot be
reduced or that the settlement of them cannot be more satisfactory, to the strikers as well as to the capitalist. After all, the
interests of the owner of a factory and of the men who work in
it are identical, and the prosperity of any community owes as
much to the ingenuity and direction of the owner as to the
industry of his employes. It is absurd to defame every capitalist
as a merciless and mercenary autocrat, wolfishly rapacious,
tyrannizing over innocent and credulous men, exploiting them,
draining their energies and wearing away their lives, with no
thought except for his own belly and his own purse. And it is
equally false to howl down every mill hand as an ignoramus, a
bestial lout, valueless to society, unable to conduct his own life,
and fit for nothing but victimization by a ruthless factory routine. What is needed is more light, more knowledge on both
sides, for strikes arise out of misunderstanding. The employe
must know the problems as well as the objectives of his employer and realize the relations which exist between the industry
at which he works and raw materials, markets, and wars. So,
too, must the employer make an effort to understand the handi-
caps of his men, their points of view, their necessities, their
desires; he must comprehend that even though his interests and
theirs in the successful functioning of his plant are the same,
yet there are points at which his material interests and theirs
cross, and that, in such a crossing, their interests are paramount
because they are those "of civilization and the community."
Only if he is sympathetic to them and they to him, only if they
willingly co-operate and make mutual concessions can anything approaching industrial harmony exist in the future.
Without such rational conduct, chaos will prevail. "This may
sound vague," Morley himself admitted, but panaceas have no

place in the experience of men, and dreams of ideal systems, despite their beauty, are worthless.

Yet, even though "all the people in the world are not sensible, patient, unprejudiced" and invariably careful in their conduct, most of them, workers as well as capitalists, can be taught to assume a reasonable and beneficial amount of "moral responsibility to the commonwealth," and it was this assumption alone which, Morley felt, would enable his country to weather the "great economic revolution" sooner or later to convulse western Europe and possibly even to strike "tranquil, conservative and unspeculative England." In Socialism, he had no confidence. It was a panacea, of a special political kind, whose weakness lay in its attempt to impose a pattern on men from the outside instead of beginning by reforming them inside, and in a sentence which might have come from his revered Burke he declared that "no political solution is adequate for a mighty problem that is at once economic and moral."[2] Socialism was not a dying or doomed force, however. About its torch, still alight in western Europe, in spite of his disapprobation he was concerned enough to ask whether it burned for illumination or conflagration. Solutions of the dominant problem of industrial organization varied, after all; there was no one system which would do for all the nations of western Europe. Socialism might conceivably be the "wholesome and normal type" for Russia, say, or France; but England was not therefore bound to adopt it. For her a partial displacement and gradual modification of the old feudal structure was best, because the capitalist performed "functions with which the workmen will never be able to dispense." In the period of transition and alteration, how-

---

[2] Morley's aversion to panaceas is exemplified, too, in his abhorrence of economic catchwords, phrases, and theories. Particularly irksome to him was the ubiquitous mouthing of "supply and demand" and the application of it as a formula by advocates of unlimited production. "Unlimited production implies illimitable demand, which is an absurdity." Since foremost political economists were speculators who could not agree with one another, he saw no reason why laborers' minds should be befuddled with their jargon.

ever, all laboring people should form vigorous unions for themselves, whose continual pressure on capitalists would stimulate the growth in them of the requisite "social and moral motives."

As to the desirability of unions, Morley had not the least doubt. But their advantage lay not only in their being a means for bettering wages; more important was their service in accustoming workers to co-operating with one another. Without the habit of acting in concert with his fellows, of subordinating personal aims and desires to the good of a whole community, no man was "more than half a human creature." Although Parliamentary elections were too infrequent and Parliament itself too far removed from mill hands and miners for them to be strongly and continually attentive to national affairs, their unions gave them a field of social and political activity that was immediate; their day-to-day awareness of belonging to a great combination was "like belonging to a great country."

To the question whether workmen were capable of such realization, Morley had early answered in a stout affirmative. After all, labor unions, like political elections and political parties and political constitutions, were what Matthew Arnold asserted them to be—machinery and nothing more. He had seen eye to eye with Arnold in this from the start. What really mattered was the men who composed unions and parties, was what they thought and how they acted with one another. It was imperative for the salvation of democratic society that all workers, now that they had obtained political power, should have inculcated in them the ideas and affections which would fit them to wield their power intelligently and for their own good. Since the landed and commercial plutocracy was too "choked by wealth" to point a way into the future, since the church as a force was impotent, and since newspapers were too much the instruments of capitalist controllers and too responsible to their advertisers, the great body of laborers was left as the only hope of England. All his life Morley protested against calling artisans "roughs." True, they had neither the time nor the means for solving the complicated problems of government; but a workman, he insisted, no more needed a course in political economy than a farmer did one in geology or astronomy. "If the facts are put honestly before them," he affirmed, "I would trust any great popular body of our countrymen—and the greater the body, the more sure would my trust be—to decide upon them with generosity, with straightforward manly simplicity."

Morley's conduct with laborers was marked by admirable honesty, candor, and common sense. But in this as in so many other things, he was only being consistent with lines of behavior that he had drawn for himself back in the first years of his apprenticeship. Before he was twenty-seven he had seen enough of it to denounce the hypocrisy of upper-class reformers who exhorted artisans to do one thing and then did the opposite themselves. He was obdurate in flaying cant. Class distinction in relaxation and recreation, in spite of the sophistries of demagogues, was good; and so, although he was an advocate of workmen's clubs, he disapproved of their being turned into pleasureless Sunday school rooms on the one hand, or soft lounging places on the other, where rich sympathizers could come and practice, *en bonhomme*, an artful fraternizing. As editor of *The Fortnightly* he was in some demand to speak before laboring groups; always he exercised a judicious clearsightedness as to the difference between his station and theirs, his function and theirs. He never put on a show; he never talked down. Though he could remind an audience of miners that ideas are sometimes as hard to get at as coal or limestone and that fatigue can follow prolonged mental exertion, too, he dismissed as "nonsense and clap-trap" the notion that there was no distinction between him and them. Nevertheless it was a good thing, he held, for both kinds of men to see as much as possible of one another; and he welcomed an occasion of speaking to them as an unanswerable refutation of the contention of "preposterous alarmists" that the continued growth of industrial unions would drive all intelligent, self-respecting men out of the field of politics and leave it to slick-tongued, unscrupulous demagogues. If such men did disappear from public life, it would be through their own fault.

Although politics were no cure-all but only a special kind of machinery, a political form was valuable in facilitating certain social improvements. The regeneration and salvation of England rested upon the leavening and shaping of human character, it was true, but any reformer too impetuous to take notice of the irresistible modification of the English political pattern and chart his own program accordingly was venting wind to no purpose. The signs of the times all pointed in one direction—to Industrialism from Territorialism. Along that passage political progress lay; the day of a landed aristocracy with its machinery of landlords, rents, and tenantry was past. Put in another way, the future of England was dependent upon the outcome of the showdown fight between culture and democratic opinions on the one hand, and wealth and vested interest on the other—between brains and numbers, in short. Although England alone among world powers had not endured an upheaval in the twenty years between 1858 and 1878, absence of internecine turmoil was not to be interpreted as torpid impotence. The New Revolution had been under way for decades; and Morley derided old ladies who still thought dreamily about the imminence of democracy in terms of "the guillotine and Marie Antoinette," fashionable Tory hostesses who supposed vaguely that its advent would "cause Mr. Gladstone, Mr. Disraeli, Mr. Bright, and the others to chew tobacco, and to shoot at one another across the House with revolvers," and specimens of aristocratic petrifaction who were convinced that all educated men would abjure Parliament from now on and only leaders of Trades' Unions squat there to "repudiate the National Debt, secularize the revenues of the Church, and confiscate the land and the factories."

In spite of the myopia of such troglodytes the first step in the New Revolution had already been accomplished in the Reform Bill of 1867. With the definitive transference of political power from a class to the nation, the "first campaign" in the war against Privilege and Obstruction had been successfully terminated. The peaceableness of the transaction was proof that the New Revolution was only Evolution after all, unless what was now only resentment and disagreement among the classes in opposition became in time fixed hostility, and obstacles were thrown into the path of the party of Progress which could not be removed except by force. Then blood might be spilled. In answer to the die-hards who lamented that democracy would weaken the English executive, Morley explained that for years that executive had been the "weakest and most impotent . . . in the civilized world." If one wanted to see what an executive could amount to under a democratic system, one had only to consider the United States, where, during the Civil War, Lincoln had carried on "an enterprise of colossal magnitude with a vigour and completeness and clearness of practical vision only to be paralleled in English history by the dictatorship of Cromwell and the dictatorship of the first and greater Pitt." The weakness being exposed by democracy in the English machinery was in the House of Lords, whose "antics" were more and more showing them up for what they were—the "recognized centers of political opaqueness."

Nevertheless, Morley knew and preached that there was nothing in the nature of things that made a democracy superior to an aristocracy. Unless widespread apathy and sluggishness and superficiality in things political were reduced among the English, there would be a bitter reckoning to pay. Grim dangers lay ahead and it was well that the people should know about them.

Birth is as likely to give us good legislators and administrators as deliberate elections, unless the electors keep steadily in view the choice of the best man they can possibly find. An aristocracy, even demoralized as ours has become, is much more likely to produce men with the gift of government than a plutocracy, equally demoralized and timorous, and without the great advantage of good traditions.

Moreover, in spite of its usual tendency to indifference and complacency, a democracy was its own danger in its susceptibility to violence, injustice, and imperiousness, in which its extremes were as reprehensible as those of any military dynasty. Consider, Morley advised, the vindictiveness in the decree of the Athenian Demos against Mytilene, or the chauvinistic approval by the American people of the flagitious Indirect Claims. Plato's figure describing the dual nature of the soul could be applied as well to society. And the machinery of party government, too, inseparable from a democratic system, was liable to set in motion certain evils endangering society. Party wrangling, with its heinous name-calling, its recrimination, its vilification, its gutter nose-thumbing, caused open and broad controversy among statesmen to degenerate into "the spiteful scuffling of pigmies"; it was an irreparable waste of force— of governing force in rulers and moral force in people. Party craft and unscrupulousness were a further threat, for through chicanery, bribery, artful misrepresentation, and demoralizing money squandering, mediocrities were boosted into legislative office who were nothing but tools. Too many national representatives were made through such means and were narrow, servile, corrupt.

Such perils, however, did not alter the fact that a unique and immeasurable advantage resided in a democratic structure of society. "What we see every day with increasing clearness," Morley wrote encouragingly, "is that not only the well-being of the many, but the chances of exceptional genius, moral or intellectual, in the gifted few, are highest in a society where the *average* interest, curiosity, capacity, are all highest." This was the matchless value of a democracy: that in its encouragement and stimulation of the whole people to improve itself, it multiplied the chances of emergence of the specially endowed few who could become wise leaders. For Morley was not, any more than Mill, a leveller—unless levelling could be construed as up instead of down, even in which case he would probably have made reservations before committing himself. For him the supreme task of far-sighted statesmanship was not in establishing social equality but in creating social unity. Intent himself on capturing "the genuine air and manner of distinction," he knew well enough that not just anybody, because he was anybody, was capable of living up to the precepts of Mill's "On Liberty." The cultivation of complete independence and true individuality requires extraordinary discipline of will and intellect. For this reason he could say that that essay was "in fact one of the most aristocratic books ever written," taking the pains to add that he did not mean "British aristocratic, 'with the politest and gracefullest kind of woman to wife.' "

In the long run Morley believed that democratized constituencies of working men would see England safely through her crisis. Theirs was a sure but inexplicable instinct (a mystery to anybody except believers in democracy) for feeling and sympathizing with the right cause. Possessing an advantage at the outset in being unencumbered by "fixed ideas" and moving in the "bracing air of common life," once their native hard-headedness and common sense were sharpened and informed by education, they would own "as much of the information necessary for shaping a sound judgment on the political issues submitted to them, as an equal number of average Masters of Arts and Doctors of Laws." They could always be relied upon to choose the best man in debate, to see through and reject the candidate who, in the face of "a vast host of new difficulties" came equipped "with only the old clumsy and ineffectual weapons."

The political existence of England, however, was not confined within the shores of the British Isles, unrelated to and unaffected by the daily life of nations elsewhere in the world. Nothing more outraged Morley's political conscience than the time-worn asseveration that, because of her geographical insularity, England could pursue, and profitably, a policy of isolation. Whether they wanted to or not, the English people must realize that their country was a vital organ in the great world body politic, for the healthful and efficient functioning of which English participation and co-operation were essential. To think otherwise was absurdity and delusion. As though in the human body the heart could suddenly declare itself independent of all other organs and attempt to follow an exclusive path of operation! Moreover England could not afford to remain indifferent to what happened in other parts of the globe for the elementary reason that her possession of widely scattered dependencies linked her willy-nilly with the activities of other continents, imposed upon her international obligations which she was powerless to disregard. In the matter of India, for example, it was her duty, first to govern India for the Indians, efficiently and beneficently, but also to cultivate and maintain friendliness with the nearest great power, Russia. And so, years later as England's Secretary of State for India, Morley himself was to be influential in effecting an entente with Russia to relieve his anxiety over the Indian frontier.

England's imperialism was a thorn in Morley's flesh, and he condemned it incessantly for a "silly policy." In the first place it was a perpetual incitement to greed, which viciously, with the acquisition of every new colony, only whetted men's appetites to reach out and grab another. Unending conquest and inordinate exploitation were its poisonous fruits. It was shameful of England, the most civilized nation in the world, to set an example of rapacity and callous inefficiency by stirring recklessly abroad and encumbering her hands with extraneous responsibilities while urgent problems by the score demanded her whole attention at home. She should set her own house in order before undertaking to teach other peoples how to live. In their secret moments of candor, what guilt must imperialistic statesmen own to, not manful enough to proclaim openly what he was preaching in his *Fortnightly*, that "the crust of a seared conscience is a perilous base for an empire"! Irresponsible exemplars of the patriotism that is only "canting and insolent nonsense," in 1879 they forced on the African Zulus a war which was "one of the worst crimes . . . ever . . . perpetrated" in England's history. Let them remember Spain and Portugal, whose brutality in founding and treating colonies overseas only "strewed a hemisphere with such states as Mexico, drifting and festering like a Leviathan wreck on the tideless heavy waters of that worst barbarism which comes of the corruption of civilization." Moreover, England should abandon imperialism because her populace had lost its longing for a world-wide empire on which the sun would never set. This part of the handwriting on the wall, Morley had read with finality as early as 1875. And beyond that, climactically, was his conviction that imperialism was incompatible with a democratic form of government. After all, an imperialistic policy was one constantly precipitating emergencies, and did anybody suppose that the slowness of parliamentary procedure was fitted for the quick action which they demanded?[3] More than that, could it be

---

[3] Thirty-three years later, however, Morley was of the mind that "empire over distant dependencies has not been broken down by democracy at the metropolis" but by absolutism in one form or another; and he cited the disintegration of the Roman and Spanish empires, as well as the severing of the thirteen American colonies from

imagined that the power of variable constituencies was reconcilable with a program of continual aggrandizement? If France had had household suffrage during the Napoleonic era, was it likely that those prolonged wars would have been fought?

England's extra-insular relations were not restricted, however, to the colonial members of her empire. Other independent nations in the world, in particular the nations of continental Europe, demanded careful attention, for since their spheres of economic, scientific, and aesthetic activity were continually intersecting England's own, it was preposterous to think that she could disregard their political movement. Russia, for example, was much more a force than people imagined; sooner or later the world would have to reckon with her. Morley feared her smoldering might and considered with dread the "anarchic conservatism" which would overtake Central Europe if the "half-barbarous Russian swarms" burst through their western walls. About Germany, even after the Franco-Prussian War, his ideas were progressive and hopeful. Her unification and preponderating was a prerequisite to any stability on the continent and the only sure barrier to Russian incursion; he welcomed it. Since it was strictly a consummation of the political desires of the whole German nation, it was inevitable; whereas the effort of France to dominate was the expression solely of the detestably selfish dynastic aspirations of one corrupt man, Louis Napoleon. To be sure, Germany exhibited military cruelty and the barbarous principle of divine right, but she was still in a transitional, semi-feudal state; once she had achieved maturity and integration, she would devote her energies to civilization, to Liberalism. France, temporarily "the great high temple and shrine of piratical Bonapartism," was the bearer

their mother country, to warn twentieth-century Britons that wise rule in India would be "overthrown by the folly of democracy" in the British Isles. See "British Democracy and India," *Nineteenth Century,* LXIX (February, 1911), 189-209.

of a mission that was, after all, "spiritual rather than material; intellectual rather than military."

Since he was confident that the era of militarism was drawing to an end and western civilization was on the threshold of an epoch of pacific industrialism, in which the domestic happiness of peoples everywhere would supplant territorial conquest as the supreme objective of national policy, Morley advocated a voluntary assumption by England of leadership in the new international order. England was the most advanced industrially among all countries, and the most wealthy; she, therefore, knew most acutely the losses to be suffered in an outbreak of wars. Her cause, more than the cause of any other power, was the cause of peace; and her chief function should be to spread harmony and understanding among occidental lands, as her chief self-imposed obligation already was to sow the seeds of civilization in savage places. Her "international duty" was to intervene in Europe. Abstinence from aggression, while it was something, was not enough, for were there not sins of omission as well as of commission? England must become "the high-minded, benignant, and virile guardian of the European peace." Only so could she justify her high position among nations and demonstrate that she was not following "both riches and peace in a base fashion." Three years before the Franco-Prussian War, Morley deplored that his country had not used the force of her navy and military armament to keep down continental aggressors, to make France and Germany behave. He pleaded with statesmen to discontinue the age-old policy of contracting alliances on geographical principles and effect them thenceforth only on moral grounds. If it were seen, after faithful study, that Russia, for instance, in the temper of her national life, bore much in common with England, that the lines of social development into the future ran parallel for both countries, then an alliance should be made with her.

Morley's aversion to war and militarism did not mean that

he was unpatriotic. As leader of *The Fortnightly Aufklärung*, he distinguished his own reasoned patriotism on the one hand, with its sense of justice to other nations and its clear perception of the real interests for England, from that "pagan" chauvinism on the other which listened only to "hollow blasts" on "the trumpet of patriotic charlatanry" and puffed itself with superstition and prejudice. Militarism was only "fatuous soldiering" and the fondness of a good many people for it was what had brought about the "silly military panic" after the German crushing of France in 1871. A spreading of militarism with its supplanting of "civil liberty by the license of martial law," would result in something to be envisioned with horror—a transformation of the old England of justice and freedom "into a Pirate-Empire, with the Cross hypocritically chalked upon its black flag."

Although the Franco-Prussian struggle modified Morley's views on war, it did not unrecognizably warp their shape. In 1875 he believed as fervently as he had in 1867 that it was England's great moral responsibility to take the leadership among nations in an effort to make peace prevail, only he no longer advocated her intervening by herself as supreme policeman. For the future she must organize a great league of pacific powers to include Italy, Austria, Belgium, Turkey, and to be equipped to reinforce diplomacy by military sanctions. Only through such a determined, concerted effort could recalcitrant potential belligerents be kept down and the flames of war smothered. But such international co-operation must be tough-fibered; it must consist of more than self-satisfying assiduousness in exchanging notes and making promises. As Morley put it,

It is worse than puerile if all our inspired leading articles about the strength of England, the resoluteness of England, the great virtuousness of England, the fine place of England in Europe, only mean that one of our ambassadors is occasionally to read out Aesop's fable of the Wolf and

the Lamb, done into diplomatic phrase by Lord Derby, for the benefit of
the German or other foreign minister. . . .

Pious didacticians who believed that a canting of the "vague
and unreal moralities of the old religion" would dispel notions
of war were deluding themselves; so were economist-statisti-
cians who cited the intricacy of international trade relations
and the increases resulting to England from a lowering of her
tariff barriers. It was true that England had opened her markets to the world; but since man cannot live by bread alone, let
her now open her heart as well.

And it was exactly this opening of the heart everywhere, this
"new and enlarged illumination of the social sentiment" all
over the world that was the only sure means to quenching the
fires of international hatred, the only real foundation for a
lasting peace. It underlay even Morley's plan, his machinery,
for a league of pacific powers to enforce peace. After all, there
can be no war only if a people will not have it. An enlightened
populace is the only supreme arbiter, the sole guarantee against
war. So in every nation people must have their conceptions of
what constitutes public duty and public benefit broadened.
They must see beyond arbitrary political boundaries, transcend
primitive race prejudice, and convert chauvinism into broad
civilized sympathy and obligation. Devoid of such intellectual
agreement, such moral unity, such commonness of sentiment,
an international league would be foredoomed to early dissolution, for its members would have no reason and no means for
perpetuating their accord. There had been one period in European history when such understanding and amity among nations was being realized. From the end of the Seven Years' War
to the French Revolution, when the "better side of French
thought" was pervading western Europe, there was a growth of
tolerance, of what might have become an almost universal
disinclination to war, but Napoleon ended it by sowing the
seeds of an intensified, poisonous international rivalry such as

Europe had never known before. Looking into the future, Morley could see that without a universal informing and transforming of common opinion (far more than an "uncolored and nerveless cosmopolitanism") no peace would be any more than that of 1871, "a more or less prolonged truce" which the belligerents used only to recover their breath and reconsolidate their forces for another swift, desperate, and sanguinary struggle. Prophetically, he warned against the time when Germany might seize not only France but Holland and Belgium as well in a "monstrous pacification." What human beings must realize is that wars are not necessary in every small quarrel to express national disapproval or impose chastisement. In most such instances "reprobation by public opinion" should be resorted to and would prove sufficient. The true mark of the civilization of any country is the degree of moral force it can exert, not the quantity of military force it can muster. In this respect it would be well to emulate America, who, with inferior armament, already exercised more moral power over France and Germany than England herself. And so Morley in 1870 exhorted public opinion not only in England but in all Europe to consolidate itself and sternly censure Germany for her seizure of Alsace. With "no natural gift" for turning his "cheek to the smiter," he would not assert that war is never necessary, never "justifiable";[4] in fact, the American Civil War was one struggle which he never tired of saying could not have been averted by any amount of diplomacy. Still he maintained that war is so hideous and so far-reaching and deadly, psychologically as well as materially, that it ought to be more carefully considered, weighed, and guarded against than any other incident in a nation's life. As for England herself, he was sure that in the future, so influential and peaceful were her enfran-

[4] In 1901, after condemning the Boer War, he nevertheless averred that there are some situations when war is a national duty, not to be shirked without dishonor. "I have no natural gift, I am sorry to say, of turning my cheek to the smiter." Sirdar Ali Khan, *The Life of Lord Morley* (London: Pitman and Sons, Ltd., 1923), p. 163.

chized workers, any prime minister who attempted to engage her in a long war would have to show "with unanswerable force of demonstration, and often repeated, that the very independence of the country" was in danger, or else "overthrow the electoral system."

III

It was during the *Fortnightly* period that Morley, in the attainment of his full intellectual stature, first reached a height where he could measure John Stuart Mill and discern deficiencies in his thinking. He venerated Mill, not only for his wisdom but for his benignity; his was a lofty moral intelligence. And although he came to see as he grew older that what had appeared at Oxford to be the star's brilliance of Mill's philosophy, the world considered more nearly a lamp's glow, he never ceased to recognize the wisdom in it. In Parliament in 1906 he lovingly cited the last chapter in Mill's work on representative government as "still the classic book on the subject."

Most of his divergences from the path of the great Utilitarian were on the subject of religion and were occasioned by the appearance in 1874 of Mill's *Three Essays On Religion*. Mill's pronouncements were a stimulus, an excitation, and forced him to re-examine his whole structure of ideas on theology. Because Mill had admitted that on the grounds of worldly evidence, a divine revelation, in the case of Christ and his mission, was not impossible or incredible, and furthermore that, on the grounds of evidence, although there is no assurance of life after death, there is at the same time nothing to forbid or prevent anybody from believing in such a state, if he feels the belief "conducive either to his satisfaction or his usefulness," Morley immediately ascribed to him a "creed of low probabilities and faintly cheering potentialities." Then, after explaining that the best way of showing respect to one's best teacher was in not veiling or muffling one's "strong dissent," and after acknowledging his own intellectual inferiority, he launched into a deploring of Mill's "obliqueness, evasiveness," and "shiftiness of issue" in the whole controversy. He was perplexed and disappointed by Mill's failure to say exactly what he meant by religion, and he contradicted point-blank Mill's opinion—"When the only truth ascertainable is that nothing can be known, we do not, by this knowledge, gain any new fact by which to guide ourselves." What lamentable ambiguity there was, too, in Mill's avowal that it is "perfectly conceivable that religion may be morally useful without being intellectually sustainable"! Useful to whom? To an individual if he himself cannot sustain it and has therefore ceased to believe in it? Or to other people while they have not yet discovered that it cannot be defended? In that case, if they do not know it to be false, it is still intellectually sustainable to them. As for Mill's speaking of God as a Mind—how could Mind, even though spelled with a capital, be an entity? On the one hand, to imagine that mind can have existence apart from body is to run perilously close to the abstruseness of "Plato's doctrine of archetypal Ideas," and on the other, to endow a supernal mind with body is to be anthropomorphic. Finally, in spite of having taught for years that there was no evidence in Nature of a benevolent creator, Mill had backtracked in this last book and admitted evidence, after all, of a creator benevolent, even though not wholly so. What an apostasy!

In addition to these religious differences there were several other minor qualifications which details of Mill's thought underwent in Morley's mind. One of the weakest points in Mill's doctrine of liberty was, he said, "the extreme vagueness of the terms protective and self-regarding." How can any opinion or any serious act be regarded as wholly, unreservedly self-regarding? More penetrating thinking and more sharp definition were needed here. Mill's exposition of Utilitarianism, too, was marred by a shortcoming. He had said that the motive of a doer of an act has nothing to do with the morality of his act. Morley, strenuous in his reasoning, disagreed. In spite of his great deference to the man who had "done so much to reconstruct and perfect the utilitarian system," he was constrained to show that the doer has to be included among all those on whose happiness his act has any effect, for, since "his motive reacts with full power upon his character, strengthening or weakening this or that disposition or habit" in it, the results of that motive on himself have to be considered among the total consequences of the act.

What is significant, however, is that in spite of these disagreements with parts of Mill's doctrine, these specialized refinements of it, Morley remained faithful to the body of it to the end of his days. He never denied that the most desirable thing for society is the development of aristocratic individuals, independent in mind, disciplined in will, and cultivated in taste; and his own life bore admirable testimony to the degree to which, in a commoner, aristocratic individualism can rise. And since in his sight a democratic political organization afforded the most channels of cultivation to the most individuals, like Mill he clung to democracy and shunned Socialism.[5] His

---

[5] Mill's feelings about Socialism require some explanation. In an uncompleted book on the subject, published after his death (at Morley's urging) by his wife in *The Fortnightly*, XXV (February, March, April, 1879), as "Four Chapters on Socialism," he rejected Socialism as a politico-social form adoptable by the English nation. "The evils and injustices suffered under the present system," he wrote, "are great, but they are not increasing; on the contrary, the general tendency is towards their slow diminution." No one abuse existed, he held, the simple abolition of which would land humanity in a state of happiness. The answer to the question whether a capitalistic or a Socialistic state offered the better chance "for overcoming the inevitable difficulties of life" was far more dependent on "intellectual and moral conditions" than most people imagined. The chief evil of Socialism he saw as the "delusive unanimity produced by the prostration of all individual opinions and wishes before the decree of the majority."

On the other hand, Leslie Stephen, in his *The English Utilitarians* (Vol. III, pp. 224-29), shows that Mill, by making concession after concession to state regulation of the conduct of individuals, had gone step by step farther toward Socialism than his aversion to it all-of-a-piece would indicate possible.

belief in an enlightened minority was the rock on which he built his faith for living; without it there was only dust.

Crowded and busy as Morley's *Fortnightly* days were with editing, writing, and speaking, there was time nevertheless for diversions, for graces and refinements. Plays, operas, oratorios, and recitals gave continual satisfaction. Trips to the continent were stimulating, through a change of scene, making of new friends, and firsthand observing of foreign political developments. Luncheons with companions and evenings with guests at home remained durable pleasures. And there were visits to especial intimates like Leslie Stephen or George Meredith or Mill himself, from which he would come away refreshed and happy but somewhat saddened, too, because to his elegiac nature even "the most delightful days" were, "like all other days, delightful and sorrowful." Sometimes it was his good fortune to play Boswell to Mill and take down to Blackheath some eminent person who had never met the great Utilitarian. On one occasion, Mill having expressed a desire to make the acquaintance of Trollope, Morley arranged to convoy the novelist down on a Sunday afternoon. But in spite of Trollope's assurance beforehand, "Stuart Mill is the only man in the whole world for the sake of seeing whom I would leave my own home on a Sunday," the party was not a success. Trollope proved to be a bull in a china shop; his blustering impinged cacophonously on Mill's gentle courtesy and modesty. Morley was relieved to get his guest safely away. "Trollope," he concluded, "did not recognize the delicacy of Truth, but handled her as freely and as boldly as a slave-dealer might handle a beautiful Circassian." Often, in the drawing room of George Eliot and G. H. Lewes, when the serious talk about Comtism had run its course, Lewes himself, "a source of incessant and varied stimulation," would cast a bohemian fascination over the company and reminisce vivaciously though somewhat shockingly about his early days in second-rate theaters. Or Trollope, again, would make the floor shake with his bawling voice as he told a funny yarn or illustrated a favorite notion. For the making of a writer, he put much more faith in a lump of cobbler's wax on the seat of a chair than in inspiration, and one afternoon he "expounded this theory of the seat of inspiration . . . with an inelegant vigour of gesture that sent a thrill of horror through the polite circle there assembled"! Sunday morning breakfasts around town, where the food was abundant and the talk long, afforded recreation, but at these Morley was not always conspicuous for his voice. One morning in March, 1877, at Lord Houghton's, when the breakfast guests included a young writer from America, he was curiously silent the whole while. Henry James was impressed by his youthful appearance, thought he had "a most agreeable face," but was disappointed that "he hardly opened his mouth."

Morley's whole conductorship of *The Fortnightly* was marked by self-respecting discipline and an insistence on the highest standards. Since he had never "brutalized" the "literary ideal" himself in descending to write stuff for a publisher just to prevent him from going to another contributor for it, so he never asked any young man eager to submit material, to smirch his integrity by writing what he did not believe. Likewise, since he had early learned not to hand in "obscure and befouled manuscript," discovering it to be usually the smaller author who exploited the indecencies of illegibility, he was intolerant of procrastination and dirty scrawling in any of his own would-be contributors. "Dawdling, slipshod habits of work" were no less disgraceful in writers than in other workers. And he steadfastly refused to "read through every manuscript that any simpleton chose to pester him with"; it was "a waste of time absolute and unredeemed."

These exactions in his regime were more than beneficial to

The Fortnightly Review. In five years from the time he took command its circulation had almost doubled, and its owners, tenacious of their good investment, refused to sell. The man who had realized with his majority that true thrift consists in a "wise and careful outlay of money" and who many years later, as Secretary of State for India, was to "watch the expenditure of Indian revenue as the ferocious dragon of the old mythology watched the golden apples," demonstrated that for an editor scrupulousness was more than its own reward. Yet financial solvency was not all that *The Fortnightly* achieved in his hands. Its potency as a force leavening public opinion and stirring people to think has been attested by men who were growing up then. Through its pages, as later through his independent speeches and books, Morley, preaching as a "refined type" of heretical priest, exerted an influence on the generation maturing between 1870 and 1890 which makes him "fit to compare with any of the greater Victorians. Young men swore by him and found in his writings a more fervent and brilliant exposition of Liberal ideas than anywhere else except in the speeches of Mr. Gladstone."[6] To them he communicated something of his own disposition to swim against the stream. In intellectual circles, just as one "slept on Browning, Dean Milman, Cardinal Newman, 'Puseyism,' " so one "sipped neo-Christianity or atheism with John Morley";[7] *Fortnightly*ing was one constituent in the vogue of sophisticated radicalism.

Even though Morley had made a point, however, in the second year of his incumbency of proclaiming that his was not "the temper of the Jacobin and the sans-Culottist" and that the absence of past-destroying fanaticism in reformers of his day differentiated them from the French Revolutionists of a century before, his *Fortnightly* denunciations continued to be appre-

[6] See J. A. Spender, "Lord Morley, Last of Victorian Liberals," *Living Age*, CCCXIX (November 3, 1923), 207-10.

[7] Austin Harrison, *Frederic Harrison: Thoughts and Memories* (London: William Heinemann, Ltd., 1926), p. 67.

hended as signals for subversion. Even the scientist John Tyndall, eminently rational, came to include him "among the young men who fostered the delusions of Mr. Gladstone's old age" and foresaw dangerous possibilities that he "might someday play the role of a Robespierre." In vain did he contend that in the light of history England's national character was so intellectually sluggish as to prevent the smallest changes in government from being effected except by an "amount of effort so prodigious" as anywhere else to "mean a revolution." In 1870 a Colonel Chesney, "anti-republican, yet sick of the time, and looking earnestly for its remedies," again linked his name with that of Robespierre, and warned him that the current he was accelerating would not stop with embracing workmen but would become in time a "vortex of democracy" swirling lower to whip up the dregs of humanity and shoot them to the surface in a froth of insane mob rule which would sweep away the upper classes forever. In answer to an impassioned peroration urging him to desist from fomenting class hatred and "to construct, instead of teaching only how to destroy," Morley retaliated with the grand Burkean pronouncement, "No class has a monopoly of nonsense." England would move nowhere by thinking of her own people "as a vile and turbulent rabblement"; if Chesneyites really wanted to sound the depths of political stupidity and conceit, they should "fathom the opinions . . . of the clergy, the peerage, and the journalists" on such great subjects as the American Civil War, the extension of the suffrage, and Episcopalian disestablishment in Ireland. Assured Morley,

Nobody is less of a Robespierrist [than I], and nobody has been more careful to insist upon the mortal errors of method which marked the course of the French Revolution and landed it in disaster and ruin. . . . Whatever is written here in a revolutionary sense, is obviously a warning to those above and not an invitation or an incitement to those below.

Meanwhile, in occasional volumes published independently of *The Fortnightly Review*, Morley was making an author's name for himself. When the first book of his *Critical Miscellanies* appeared early in 1871, the same forbidding Robert Buchanan who was to damn the poets Swinburne and Rossetti that year in his "Fleshly School of Poetry," commended it in *The Contemporary Review* as a collection of "finely-wrought and thoroughly stimulating essays." Although Morley in his excessive zeal often lost sight of the relativity of truth, and in "his destructive criticisms on religion" destroyed nothing except "a little of the confidence" one usually felt in him, Buchanan nevertheless welcomed him, for his interest in sociology, his devotion to truth, and his compassion for mankind, "as another adherent to the blessed cause of Humanity." And by 1886, only three years after his withdrawal from *The Fortnightly*, with his collected works published in nine volumes by Macmillan's, Morley was being read with such approbation in America that one magazine, *The Dial*, considered proposing him as an intellectual model for young men. He was a "healthy moralist," exemplary in never trying to "minimize or to unduly extenuate" faults of his characters, but was regrettably a little too "radical religiously" to be an ideal guide for the younger generation. Still, wrote the reviewer, "as they stand, his writings, to those who look to literature for other than rhetorical qualities, are fascinating as Macaulay can never be again"!

The Fortnightly's fifteen years under Morley exemplify unsurpassably the apt phrase with which he described them—"rationalism without chill." Yet strenuous rationalist and director of the campaign though he was, he was, after all, fallible, as certain inconsistencies amusingly reveal. Short-tempered with impatient doubters of the religion of progress, to whom he pointed out that Humanity's millennium must necessarily be countless ages in the future, how could he reasonably advocate jettisoning Christianity for having failed to achieve a consummation in only eighteen hundred and seventy years? How could he denounce believers in a divine plan underlying the universe and at the same time subscribe unreservedly to the non-theological doctrine that the cosmos is an "intelligible array of orderly sequences," their end a civilized ultimate? How could he, in refuting Mr. Lecky, maintain that, although human beings have a "sense of moral obligation," it is "acquired and not innate," and then, in eulogizing Mr. Mill, defend "the ingenuous moral ardour which is instinctive in the best natures"? The temper with which he conducted *The Fortnightly* was, for that matter, often fundamentally inconsistent, and, ironically, his own words, written in description of the paradoxical strife of the times, summarize it best—a temper in which "even the principle of relativity becomes the base of a set of absolute and final dogmas, and the very doctrine of uncertainty itself becomes fixed in a kind of authoritative nihilism." Editorially he could damn the cowardice and the cant of the sinister army of clerics; socially he could be most agreeable to them and find their company easier than that of any other professional group. In the 1870's he became a member of the Metaphysical Club, which included such theological advocates as Gladstone and Cardinal Manning. He reached a "climax of delight" when he found himself placed one evening by his dinner host next to the Archbishop of Canterbury, and he was "tickled . . . hugely," he wrote Harrison, by noticing the "scandalised eyes" of the other guests as they followed his animated, cordial discourse with the prelate. On another occasion he informed his sister that his "lunch with the Dean of St. Paul's was marvellously pleasant," for he always got on "better with clergymen and pastors (yes—pastors non episcopal) than with anybody else." Did he remember that ten years earlier, in *The Saturday Review*, he had declared the selfish, equivocal opportunism of political trimmers, reprehensible as it was, less to be anathematized than the duplicity of "the compromising Gallio who would dine with an archbishop one day, and have half-a-dozen Essayists and Reviewers to breakfast the next morning"? What an indefensible inconsistency there was, too, between his refusal as a Utilitarian to accept the "stoic's paradox that pain is not an evil," because he knew its psychological and nervous shock made men worse, and his conduct as *Fortnightly* manifesto-maker in undertaking to disabuse men's minds suddenly, shock or no shock, because in the long run a direct rupture would brace and invigorate their understanding! Did he not hold loss of faith, along with bereavement and lasting disease, a justifiable excuse for falling into pessimism, into social apathy and inertia, states under any other circumstances abominable? Moreover, apart from theology, how irreconcilable were his derision of Carlyle's "boisterous old notion of hero-worship," an unedifying, unprofitable "half-truth," and his serene admission in contemplation of Mill that "an excessive admiration for a benign and nobly pitiful character is so attractive and so wholesome that one can have little satisfaction in searching for defective traits"!

Yet, arresting and human as these inconsistencies are in a survey of Morley's *Fortnightly* years, more important to the whole pattern of his life is his growth toward moderation of tone. "Humility," he had said, "is a rationalistic, no less than a Christian grace"; and while it is true that he had been from the first days of his enlightenment appropriately humble in his veneration of the great civilizers of the past and in his anxiety to contribute to the welfare of the future, it is yet no less true that his tone in saying so had not always been appropriately chastened and modest. The nearer he drew to middle age, however, the less combative and loud he became. At the beginning of his editorship, he could refrain only with difficulty from speaking as Sir Oracle; at the end he admitted in his "Valedictory" that, whereas a fellow "editor of a Review of great emi-

nence" considered himself the equal of "twenty-five members
of parliament," he "took a slightly more modest view" toward
his own abilities. "For the new priest of Literature," he had
learned, "is quite as liable to the defects of spiritual pride and
ambition as the old priest of the Church, and it is quite as well
for him that he should be on his guard against these scarlet
and high-crested sins." Over the many things he could wish to
have left unsaid, he consoled himself with the reflection, "Time,
happily, is merciful, and men's memories are benignly short."
Whereas, at the outset, in sounding the alarum against anonymous journalism, he had championed the signing of articles
because it would remove all masks, make for more hard hitting, and enable opponents to draw blood, at the conclusion he
confessed that the change from anonymity to signature had
"not led to one-half either of the evils or of the advantages that
its advocates and its opponents foretold." It was good, he had
come to see, for every writer to cultivate a "double mood of care
and carelessness," to be as preoccupied as possible with his
book, and as confident as possible about it, at the time of writing, but to treat it "as little seriously as possible" after it was
finished and launched. Such an attitude was best for the honesty of one's work and for one's own "mental health and self-
possession." For Morley refused to agree with Pliny that *scrib-
ere legenda* is on the same height with *facere scribenda*. How
many writers in a century can be adduced to illustrate it? he
would ask. There was not one book in a million, serious or
diverting, which was of any real concern.

As early as 1878 Morley put into print his realization that
Liberal reviews no longer enjoyed the advantage they had
possessed in the first half of the century. Their staffs were no
longer integrated by a set of common ideas or a current of common feeling; "cohesion" was gone. Although good, serviceable
writing was much more frequent than in 1805, no journalistic
group could be compared to the early *Edinburgh Reviewers*,

most of whom had been students at the University of Edinburgh, or to the old *Westminster Review*ers, who "had all sat at the feet of Bentham," or even to the *Saturday Review*ers in the 1850's, who had "rallied round" their editor and fought Philistinism. "At the present moment," he sighed, "the only motto that can be inscribed on the flag of a liberal Review is the general device of Progress, each writer interpreting it in his own sense, and within such limits as he may set for himself." By the end of his incumbency, this state of affairs was even more to be deplored. Unable, as their predecessors in James Mill's day were, to "explain in the large dialect of a definite scheme what were their aims, and whither they were going," Liberals in 1882 were confronted by perplexities just "as embarrassing" and, if anything, more numerous. In Manchesterism as a solution, for example, there was, to be sure, a certain utility, but at best it could be considered nothing more than "a number of empirical maxims." Spencerism was losing influence yearly, for it was utterly off the track. The state was intervening more and more often, more and more extensively, in the affairs of communities and individuals, and Spencer deplored that. Comtism, finally, was inadequate because too much of it was "arbitrary, accidental, or even personal"; it was too strongly Catholic to establish any relation to a country of democratic institutions and "centuries of energetic Protestantism."

Morley's growth away from Comtism is another of the salient features of his development during *The Fortnightly* period. Like Mill, he found the educational policy outlined by Comte, with its concentration of complete power in the hands of a small, dictatorial, priestlike class, incompatible with his belief in the right of the individual to free inquiry, and like him, too, he was turned away by near-disgust with certain essentials in the Religion of Humanity—its excessive veneration of women, its inclusion in its Pantheon of so many soldiers,

and its glorification of Humanity as an entity endowed an-
thropomorphically. Humanity on "the throne occupied by the
Supreme Being under monotheistic systems" was "a fantastic
decoration." The picture outraged his sense of the rational,
and he later summarized the creed as "hard, frigid, repulsive,
and untrue." Indeed as early as 1870 he had been nettled when
an article in *The Saturday Review* labeled *The Fortnightly*
"the effective and consistent organ" of the sect of Comte. What
of Mill and Spencer and Huxley, strong anti-Positivists! Of
Bagehot and Swinburne and Tyndall! No designation was
further from the truth. What *was* true was that *The Fortnightly*, "with the exception of *The Westminster Review*," was
"the only English organ in which Positivism" had been
"treated seriously and had fair play, and in which it" had
"never been attacked or defended except by competent persons."

Most significant of all, however, in Morley's growth is his
loss of faith in physical science and the emergence in him of
a hostile distrust of it. In his earlier days of aggressive endorse-
ment, he had been something of a militant adjutant in the cause
of Darwin, Huxley, and Tyndall. Yet, by 1871 his tone was
already cooling and his words had grown fewer; what England
needed, he said simply, was "respect for brains, faith in science, constant feeling after improvement." Less than two years
later he was alarmed. "Politics and the acquisition of wealth,"
he wrote, "do not constitute the only perils to the growth of
culture in England. The specialism of physical science threat-
ens dangers of a new kind." Eighteen months later still he was
lamenting the rapid superseding of the old Nature of theology
by the new Nature of physical science, because the new Darwinian Nature would reduce man and the importance of his
voluntary activity to nothing. In 1876 he began to bend every
effort to awakening people to the distinction between the physical sciences on the one hand, and the historical on the other,

developing just as rapidly. If all of England realized the importance of history, and if in every school it were stressed as it deserved to be, then his fear of "the excessive supremacy claimed for physical science," one of "the most impoverishing characteristics" of his day, would be allayed. True culture was invariably superior to mere physical science; a cultured traveller could take "just as much interest in astronomical, geological, and botanical matters" as the scientific traveller and yet "rejoice in all the historical and political connections" of places as well. But it was true culture alone which bestowed such advantages, never for a moment that specious culture which he could not cease decrying—the culture which was only a "fine name for drawing room prejudice plus literary impertinence."

With the moderation of Morley's tone, with the disappearance from it of the victorious ring of the Fire Bringer, there came a growing suspicion of the effectiveness of the fight he had been waging. He had begun as a hard-fisted gladiator, irrepressible in his intellectual strenuousness, who in his first campaigns against the church and plutocratic interests had called out "Reform!" in the voice of a man who feels himself on the threshold of a New Era. But as the smoke and the dust of the turmoil cleared, he saw the shapes of many of the old landmarks unchanged. How many real victories over Philistinism and Toryism had been won? How many conversions to the cause of Liberalism and Culture had been gained? Looking backward over the strife of his fifteen years in taking leave of *The Fortnightly*, he could smile with calm detachment. Had not much of the public interest in rooting out religious error really been only an "elegant dabbling in infidelity"? "The Agnostic," he admitted amusedly, "has had his day with the fine ladies, like the black footboy of other times, or the spirit-rapper and table-turner of our own." Yet, in spite of the fact that what he had been foremost in was more likely a tournament than a battle, there was reassurance in the fact that certain ideas, relatively unknown and whispered about as anarchic in 1867, had gained audible adherents by 1882, and that a certain stubborn opposition had been formed against blind custom and the rote of age-old convention. For it could never be denied that "whatever gives freedom and variety to thought, and earnestness to men's interest in the world, must contribute to a good end."

CHAPTER THREE

The Man of Action (1883-1914)
Gratifying a National Instinct in Politics

I

WHEN, in 1883, Morley went to the House of Commons to represent Newcastle, he was only making a move for which he had carefully prepared long in advance. Twice before, in 1868 and 1880, in Blackburn and in Westminster, he had tried unsuccessfully to win a Parliamentary seat. The act terminating his *Fortnightly* service was the consummation of a desire nursed for almost twenty years—to gratify the national instinct of activity and energy in "the conflicts of the political arena" and to prove the superiority of the man of action to the man of letters.[1] How carefully he had timed the embracing of his new career! For, indispensable as were "time and industry and the maintenance of a thoroughly open mind," one could not postpone indefinitely the hazards and uncertainties of the future to the comfortable fixities of the present. He was forty-five, and forty-five, as he had written in *The Fortnightly* in 1878, is a critical age! Are there not two momentous stages in the life of every "grave and sensitive nature"—the first, "on the threshold of manhood," when the youth shapes his creed

---

[1] Literature, Morley explained in *Voltaire*, must be rated below action, "not because written speech is less of a force, but because the speculation and criticism of the literature that substantially influences the world, make far less demand than the actual conduct of great affairs on qualities which are not rare in detail, but are amazingly rare in combination—on temper, foresight, solidity, daring—on strength, in a word, strength of intelligence and strength of character."

According to Austin Harrison, however, Morley declared that he entered politics to "try to lead men" because he knew the futility of an attempt "to reform them" through books.

Mrs. Humphry Ward reports that when Morley went to take his place in the House of Commons, he left her with this entreaty: "Don't weep for your friend; pray for him."

and establishes ideals, and the other "towards the later part of middle life," when the mature man becomes buffeted, his creed tested, and his ideals strained like saplings in a strong wind? And is not the second of these crises "the time of the grand moral climacteric," because the decision made in the face of it parts one finally and irrevocably "off among the sheep on the right hand or the poor goats on the left"? It is the course on which a man embarks at forty-five that will determine whether rampant selfishness, cynicism, and despondency are to choke out that "generous resolve of a fancied strength . . . not yet tried in the furnace of circumstance." In his own way, then, although he might not have liked to consider it so, Morley had crossed a Rubicon.

The vicissitudes of political life in a time of drastic social change are apparent. But, because Morley exemplified "vigilant tenacity" and had kept himself "in moral training," he weathered the turmoil and the apprehensions of the last two decades of the nineteenth century and the first decade of the twentieth. During the thirty-one years of his professional life he never ceased to show himself to the public, steady, judicious, human, indomitable. His career, however, was broken from time to time by interludes in which his refusal to modify his convictions lost him his seat in Parliament and made him resume the life of private citizen: he stood resolutely individual in 1886 in clinging to his advocacy of Irish Home Rule, in 1895 in opposing an Eight Hours Bill for labor, and in 1898 in damning English imperialism in South Africa. On the whole, his political life consisted of three chapters: the first, from 1883 through 1895, the Irish chapter, in which he was principally concerned with the struggle for Irish self-government; the second, from 1895 through 1910, fifteen years devoted to denouncing capitalistic imperialism and later to governing India; and the third, from 1910 through 1914, in which, comparatively inactive, he was senior member of the British Cabinet and served as its Lord President.

Politics, Morley had declared in *The Fortnightly*, "ought after all to be nothing more abstruse than good common sense." And in no other division of his political activity was the application of his own illuminating common sense more unbroken and long-lasting than in his concern for Ireland.[2] Common sense had told him early, as it had told Burke in 1775, that the only means of keeping any colonial dependency contented and healthily co-operative was through governing it for its own best interests. So it had been an administration of Ireland *for* the Irish that he had demanded summarily in his first pieces written as *Fortnightly* editor. English statesmen should consider the racial differences of the Irish people, the peculiarity of Ireland's history, the fundamental and ineradicable influence of Catholicism in the land, the special features of Ireland's geography and climate, and then desist from attempting to impose on her a harassingly alien social and intellectual pattern simply because they felt that what was good for themselves was best for their subject peoples. Morley's knowledge of Irish history was deep and thorough, and his candor compelled him to admit that it was a lamentable record of English crimes and follies. The worst of the counter-atrocities produced by Irish rage and fanaticism could be extenuated, for their fanaticism was born of desperation. Forced to endure in poverty, humiliation, and anguish decade after decade, the hunger of centuries gutted their stomachs, the thorn marks of generations stained

[2] Apropos of the Irish question, Morley had written in *The Fortnightly* for September 1868: "Underneath the surface of this, and wrapped up in it, are nearly all the controversies of principle which will agitate the political atmosphere for our time. . . . The functions of the state, the duties of property, the rights of labour, the question of whether the many were born for the few, the question of a centralized, imperial power, the question of the pre-eminence of morals in politics—all these things lie in Irish affairs." Nevertheless, momentous as it was, the Irish problem was less vast and grave for England, he felt, than the Negro problem for the United States.

their brows. The wrongs of Ireland must be redressed, and without delay. Morley swore that her "voice of lamentation" and her "steaming tale of social ill" should never find him "with ears stopped by comfort and arms folded in selfish ease."

Ireland *for* the Irish, however, was not Ireland *by* the Irish. Indeed, in *Edmund Burke* in 1867 Morley was convinced that "her installation as a corporate member of the Empire" was "the only position permanently possible for her," and he was full of praise for the efforts of William Pitt the Younger in 1785 to make her that. Twelve years later, actuated by the strong sense of political continuity and hallowed feeling for the traditions of English statesmanship which characterized him all his life, he was still measuring the policies and capacities of contemporary judges of Ireland in the light of the conduct and opinions of Burke, Pitt, and Fox. Indeed, no more than Burke, much of whose tolerant noblemindedness he had assimilated, could he be persuaded, "where a whole people are concerned, that acts of lenity are not means of conciliation." After conceding that the behavior of Parnell and his confederates in the House of Commons was more likely obstructionism of English legislation than vehement agitation for Irish, he nevertheless maintained that the only feasible solution of the Anglo-Irish problem lay in more and closer co-operation between the Parnellites and English Liberals, and he considered it ominous that "centrifugal forces" were "in the ascendant." In 1881, the next-to-last year of his *Fortnightly* incumbency, he still believed separation to "be a distinct step backwards, . . a disadvantage to Ireland itself." Although it would result in certain benefits—in endowing the Catholic clergy, for example, in denominationalizing education, and in ridding the country of foreign landlords, it would at the same time entail grievous inconveniences, in the necessary levying of a heavy tax to support an independent army and navy, and in the inescapable adoption of high tariffs, whose restrictions, for a land poor in natural resources, would ultimately prove disastrous. Harking back to Macaulay, whose words he quoted, he declared that if a fair trial revealed England and Ireland unable to "exist happily together as parts of one empire, in God's name let them separate." But a fair trial had never been granted; no honest attempt had ever been made to govern the Irish "as a distinct nationality, with views, traditions, interests, a religion, a character, all of its own."

Morley's first real service to the Irish cause came during the last three years of his *Fortnightly* editorship when he conducted a journalistic campaign in its behalf in a London newspaper, *The Pall Mall Gazette*, whose leadership he assumed in 1880. Seven years earlier his editorial fight for National Education had drawn to his side Joseph Chamberlain, the aggressive and personable Liberal from Birmingham, destined to become one of the leaders of his party. Now the two, fast friends, determined to collaborate in vigorous protest against the policy of coercion currently being followed by the English administrators of Ireland. With Chamberlain occupying a position in Gladstone's cabinet, and Morley holding the reins of the evening *Pall Mall Gazette*, the colleagues used their formidable power in directing broadsides at the English secretary for Ireland, and the foremost advocate of coercion, William E. Forster. During these three years Morley, whose *Pall Mall* headquarters were a hive of activity, got to know personally Parnell, Timothy Healy his lieutenant, and the rest of his henchmen. He ate and slept Ireland. In addition to holding continual conferences with all Irishmen who amounted to anything in Parliament, he made frequent trips to Ireland to confer with leaders there and keep his eye more closely on the pulse of conditions. Nevertheless, anxious as he was over the Irish cause, he clung to his old faith in friendly conciliation as the only practicable solution of Ireland's difficulties, unable to see any efficacy in "a separatist and independent Government" for her.

His Parliamentary independence showed in his first vote, which he cast with Parnell and the Irish members against Gladstone and the English Liberals on an amendment to the last Irish Land Act. Early in 1884, when an attempt to reduce the number of Irish members in Parliament was proposed, he was firm in his deprecation of the measure.

We should lose far more by irritating the people of Ireland than we should gain by taking seats from her for our own use. Ireland was entitled to exceptional representation, not so much on the score of geographical distance, as on that of moral distance, and the disadvantage under which her members laboured from the ignorance and prejudice of Englishmen about them, arising out of the differences of race and religion.[3]

Sometime between the occasion of this pronouncement and 1886, however, he encountered enough abuses in Ireland, and enough smoldering, swelling discontent, to make him realize that his belief in conciliation without independent government was no longer tenable. The skies were lowering and the storm was about to burst. He changed his mind decisively; it must be Home Rule or catastrophe. And so fervent was he in his conviction, so agitating in communicating it to others, that he was no small force in the conversion of the great Gladstone himself to this most radical of platforms.

Assiduously, eagerly, yet apprehensively, he continued to move back and forth between England and Ireland, alert to the slightest shift in the wind of sentiment. "The more I see of Ireland," he declared, "and the more I see of Irishmen—and I have some friends who are called Loyalists, as well as a great number who are called Nationalists—the more convinced I am that there are no people who would be more speedy to profit by a free parliamentary government." On one of his trips he was

[3] See W. J. Johnston, "Mr. Morley and Ireland," *Westminster Review* (May, 1906), for an excellent condensation of Morley's Irish record.

descending the winding drive from the administrative castle
through Phoenix Park on the route to Dublin. It was dusk and
he was on foot, alone and ruminating, near the spot where, four
years earlier, the blood of an English chief secretary had been
spilled in a brutal murder by Irish fanatics. His thoughts were
bitter. What merciless anger in those subordinated, what blind
prejudices in those dominating! What annihilating ferocity
and stupidity in the endless strife! Suddenly Healy, Parnell's
lieutenant, loomed in front of him, and a question, asked with
a hateful smile, shattered the silence: had he come from the
lair above? "Yes," Morley answered, "and I shall never set
foot in it again." Several months later, however, he re-entered
it as governmental minister, Chief Secretary for Ireland,
pledged to achieve reform through an undoing of the work of
William Pitt.

His secretaryship, unfortunately, was brief. The epochal
Home Rule Bill of 1886, in whose drafting he had been largely
instrumental, was defeated in its second reading, whereupon
Gladstone resigned and his government abandoned office. But,
although the struggle in behalf of Home Rule cost him his Parliamentary seat and seriously strained his friendship with
Chamberlain, who had stood for a modified form of coercion
in the crisis, he did not let himself be discouraged by his defeat.
The time and industry and thoroughly open mind to which he
had pledged himself would see him ultimately to victory. Even
before the Parliamentary vote on Gladstone's bill, he had
warned the House to beware of thinking "that the Irish Sphinx
would gather up her rags and immediately depart" from their
midst. The ensuing six years, a time for reconsolidating his
energies for a further attack on the obdurate prejudice of
Parliament, were anything but a quiet breathing-space, however. His zeal was redoubled, his speeches multiplied, his campaign itinerary expanded. All over England he went, and again
and again to Ireland, strong in his denunciation of pseudo-

reform bills meant to placate the Irish with "merely mock powers and a delusive responsibility." To effete British aristocrats,
"with the politest and gracefullest kind of woman to wife,"
complacent in their spurious culture of "drawing room prejudice plus literary impertinence," he protested that smooth
hands and a sweet tongue were no indications of any man's
ability to make laws. An Irish parliament undoubtedly would
be grosser-mannered than the polite body at Westminster, and
coarser-spoken, too, but its fund of sturdy common sense, its
directness, and its passionate eagerness to get things done
would enable it to govern as effectively for its purposes as any
other similarly constituted body in the world.

Morley's activities between 1886 and 1892 showed him in a
variety of moods and against diverse backgrounds. He could
be humorous when he wanted to be. Only the day after the re-
versal of Gladstone's Home Rule plans he presided and spoke
at a banquet of the Eighty Club in London, a Liberal enterprise for organizing young men to assume political responsibility. Easily, simply, whimsically, he diverted his listeners with
a parody of Antony's funeral oration from *Julius Caesar*, in
which Gladstone's umbrella, pierced with a thousand holes,
took the place of the corpse of Caesar. Often on tour he was
dazzled by an extravagance of pageantry. On February 1,
1888, when he and a political colleague were making a tri-
umphal entry into Dublin, escorted by a corps of guards from
fifteen quarters of the city, they found themselves the chief
spectacle in a procession led by fifty masters of ceremonies
and lighted by two thousand torches, with more than twenty
thousand persons—choristers, gymnasts, merchants, athletes,
fishermen—taking part. The tortuous stream of color and
noise, the bonfires, the bombastic speeches from high balconies
all testified that Morley was the man for Ireland. There were
grimmer occasions, too. In September 1890 he visited Tipperary. In characteristic Irish fashion, although there was less

pomp, there was no less hullabaloo. Before he could avoid it, he was engulfed by a seething mob on the verge of riot through the brutality and clumsiness of the police. He saw men clubbed without provocation and driven from a spot where the law allowed them to be; he saw clusters of women and children charged by mounted, helmeted guardians of Tipperary peace. Blood was spilled and his own hat was knocked off. In spite of the fact that he was later to tell the House of Commons smilingly, apropos of riot measures, that the sight of broken heads did not frighten him because he had been raised in his father's surgical office, he was indignant at the fracas and nettled by his awkward reception. When the current Chief Secretary for Ireland, Mr. Balfour, got wind of his dissatisfaction, his lip curled with the dry comment that he liked Mr. Morley better when he was writing history than when he was making it. Morley's only profit was in realizing again, and more forcibly, what he declared he had known for years: that to succeed in politics, three things are necessary—an ardent heart, a hard head, and a thick skin!

Meanwhile, in respites between lectures and tours Morley might have been found enjoying the tranquillity of his home in South Kensington. Inside his house, not at all different from a hundred others in its regular exterior, there was a collected, restful atmosphere; the cool silence that prevailed in the absence of children was so profound, said an acute French observer, Augustin Filon, that Ben Jonson's Morose would have welcomed the place as his habitation. Upstairs was the library, Morley's retreat for meditation and study. There, with one wall wholly occupied by his books, and surrounded by no *bibelots*, no vivid colors, not a single trace of affectation or the exotic, he rested, steadied his mind, fortified his will. The severity of the room, midway between banality and elegance, was distinguished by its harmony of fine, pale nuances. His predilection for a soothing whiteness, discreet and somewhat gray, was evident, and it was not to be overlooked that for him, as a thinker, such a whiteness might possess "the symbolic charm of a synthesis of colors."

In 1892, however, a new call to arms was sounded; Gladstone and his Liberals were returned to office. No time was lost. A committee of six was appointed from the Cabinet to draw up a new Home Rule Bill; and in this, Morley, acknowledged by Gladstone to be "about the best stay" he had, took a leading part. After stirring debate, the new Bill passed in its second reading before the House of Commons. In the House of Lords, unfortunately, it was killed by an overwhelming majority; and with the consequent dissolution of the Cabinet that had framed it, the cause of the crusaders for a free Ireland was dealt another discouraging blow. Morley, however, unshaken in his resolve to labor on, warned the Lords not to delude themselves with the idea that the question of Home Rule was "going to slumber," and added with flaming words that Irishmen all over the world looking to him and his co-leaders should not have their trust deceived. The Home Rule principle had "now rooted itself; the justice of the demand" was immutably established. And so, rather than sever any administrative connection with the cause even in the aftermath of the Parliamentary defeat, he strove on for three more years in a second term as Chief Secretary for Ireland. His efforts were doomed to bear no fruit, however, and his energy was wasted. In his headquarters in Dublin Castle, a "grim apartment" where he could only spend "unshining hours in saying No to impossible demands, and inventing plausible answers to insoluble riddles," his conscience troubled him; unable to forget the pledges he had made as Home Rule champion, he was too sharply aware of the ugly contradiction between them and his present executive position, in which he bore more than he wanted of the burden of responsibility for coercion. His isolation irked him, for his Nationalist friends had forsworn his company and bound themselves by oath not even to dine with him. Day after day, surrounded by numbers of complex advisory boards, and with an unsurpassable, English-created constabulary force at his disposal, he was tormented by the sight of Irish representatives condemned to stand idly by, never entrusted with the minutest responsibility or the simplest service in the government of their own country. In 1895, it was with more relief than regret that he accepted his removal from office and withdrew once more to private citizenship.

With the relinquishment of the Secretaryship and the departure from Dublin Castle, Morley was turning his back on what were, in many respects, the golden years of his career. Certainly no other time would see him so conspicuous in the front ranks of the battle, so excitingly acclaimed by those for whom he fought. The future would not shine before him with such quickening promise; nor would his hand be so near the fore in the shaping of state policy to determine it. Those were years when reason seemed an infallible guide, when it was impossible to put down the conviction that diligent application of it was the sure solution to the most perplexing of national problems. After 1895 the wheels of Britain's destiny rolled on other courses, and his attention, willy-nilly, was drawn more and more from Ireland and made to bear on more remote places of the globe.

In the last half of the 1890's with imperialism in the ascendancy, much of his strength was spent in predicting the disgrace, the disaster in store at the summit of its rise. His speeches were struck off with no less defiance of the bad, no less zeal for the good than had marked his fearless exposures during his *Fortnightly* tenure, when he had denounced England's war against the Zulus in 1879, and warned against using the Suez Canal as a pretext for exploiting Egypt in 1882. Then, in addition to abhorring imperialism for its inhumanity, he had belittled it as a "silly policy"; now he stigmatized it as a "filthy rag." He refused to give even one hurrah for the Queen's Diamond Jubilee in 1897, and he desisted even more scornfully from voting for a Parliamentary grant to Kitchener after the victory of Omdurman in 1898, maintaining that the general had "violated the Mahdi's tomb." These acts of indignant opposition did not spring at all, however, from any narrow, peevish desire to be in "a complacent minority of one"; thirty-five years earlier he had set himself to avoid falling into just that. They were prompted by the same high-souled yearning for justice that led him to inveigh against the conquest of the Sudan in 1896 because he knew that it would lead to the permanent occupation of Egypt. But it was the era of Kipling and Rhodes, and Morley, caricatured by *Punch* as Diogenes searching with his lantern for a true Liberal, found his words lost in the wind to a society "prostrate before the idol of Empire." In September, 1897 he defined bitterly and ruthlessly for his constituents at Arbroath, Scotland, the five steps in the "Forward" Rake's Progress;[4] and in January, 1899, before another Scottish audience at Brechin, he branded "manifest destiny" as "moonshine" and "war for commerce" as "murder for gain," pointing out how only three years before, Lord Roseberry, and only ten years before, Lord Salisbury, both at present leading charioteers for imperialism, had defined, respectively, a march on the Sudan as an outrage to France, and an attempt to civilize Africa as a futile waste of blood and treasury. After castigating all those who believed General Gordon's death to have been

---

[4] "First, to push on into places where you have no business to be, and where you had promised you would not go; second, your intrusion is resented, and in these wilds resentment means resistance; third, you instantly cry out that the people are rebels and their act is rebellion, in spite of your assurances that you had no intention of setting up a permanent sovereignty over them; fourth, you send forces to stamp out the rebellion; fifth, having spread bloodshed and confusion and anarchy, you declare with hands uplifted to heaven, that moral reasons force you to stay, for if you were to leave, this territory would be left in a condition no civilized power would contemplate with equanimity and composure." This whole speech can be found in the appendix of Morley's *Speeches on Indian Affairs*.

avenged by the slaughter of 10,000 Moslems at Omdurman (as though Gordon were "some implacable pagan deity who needed to be appeased by hecatombs of human sacrifice"), he went on to deride the clergy, Christian apologists for the war in Africa. A "sinister clerical army of 28,000 men in masks," he had called them years before. And indeed here they were now declaring that there were, after all, worse things than war, that even a Christian could not afford to stand for peace at any price! What if a doctor simply shrugged his shoulders and sat down apathetic in front of his patient with the remark that what was, was, and that there were worse things than smallpox and delirium tremens! Morley had no difficulty at all in imagining the clergy in company with the Forty Thieves and in hearing them say that they were for the Ten Commandments, to be sure, but that it was still a work-a-day world, and, since they could not stand "aloof from the practical business of life," they could hardly be for the Ten Commandments at any price.

By 1904, however, the temper of the imperialists had cooled considerably, and the star of imperialism was itself sufficiently on the wane to enable Morley to relax in his vigilance against it. An invitation from his good friend Andrew Carnegie urged him to visit America, not only to deliver the Founder's Day address at the Carnegie Institute in Pittsburgh, but also to observe the coming presidential election and to accompany the Carnegies to the World's Fair in St. Louis. Inasmuch as it had been thirty-seven years since his other Atlantic crossing, he accepted eagerly. In the United States he met Elihu Root, "the most satisfactory American statesman" he had yet seen, and spent several days with Theodore Roosevelt in the White House, the president and Niagara Falls remaining in his mind as the "two wonders" in the land. Publicly he distinguished himself by his Founder's Day address at the Institute estab-

lished by his host.[5] With no pretense at being apocalyptic, with
none of the pose of the seer, he nevertheless let his mind range
over the centuries and tried to discern the growth in values of
the civilization that had evolved. For his theme was progress,
and the relation to it of democracy—old subjects, both, but no
less profound for all his years of preoccupation with them, and
touched this time with a newness of phrase, a questioning sympathy of tone that revealed his complete humanity.

The assimilation of so many heterogeneous alien groups and
the fusion of them into such a great, industrialized, and apparently pacifically ordered society was an accomplishment of the
United States not to be rivaled by the most celebrated acts of
the Roman Church or the Byzantine Empire or Russia or any
of the most powerful despots who had ever lived. But the en-
abling of millions of hitherto incompatible foreigners to speak
English was not in itself progress. What was tragically essential was that the Anglicized millions all over the world, in striving "with peoples of other tongues and other stock for the
political, social, and intellectual primacy among mankind,"
strive only "in lofty, generous, and never-ceasing emulation."
Progress was not a certainty, and to think so was a superstition,
a fatalism that could not but weaken the sense of individual
responsibility. As for defining it, who could fathom its secret?
Morley was "not bold enough to try"; the complicated and
delicate relationship of moral advance to material improvement
was baffling. Too often, when physical hardships of living
were removed, intellectual or nervous harassments usurped
their place. In the sphere of government, however, where democracy was already being challenged and its claim to supremacy among political forms denied, he was standing his ground
against all pat mathematical objections that it was a violation

---

[5] "Some Thoughts on Progress," *Educational Review*, XXIX (January, 1905).
The speech is provocative, timely and timeless for any democracy, and written in
Morley's best later-day style. It should be disinterred and brought to light in a new
publication.

of liberty because under it half a community plus one could oppress half a community minus one; "so far as experience has yet gone, a modern community as a whole is likely to be a great deal better off under the rule of half its numbers plus one than it would be under the rule of one minus the half." Whether democracy would make for peace, however, everybody had yet to see; undeniably, in Europe it had done little to retard "the turbid whirlpools of a military age." What human beings everywhere must remember was that, though "all politics are a rough second best," human effort must not slacken and allow them to degenerate into a third best or no best at all. Above all, men and women should "keep free of that fatal source, even in superior minds, of mental impoverishment, that comes of expecting more from life and the world than the world and life have to give"; year after year they should inexorably "demand the uttermost" from themselves.

Back in England in 1905, Morley soon found the page opened on a new chapter in his political career. In a Liberal cabinet formed by his friend Sir Henry Campbell-Bannerman, he was appointed to the important post of Secretary of State for India. India was more and more being regarded as England's insoluble problem, but Morley, who held insoluble problems to be only problems wrongly stated, undertook his new duties with confidence and enthusiasm. He was not unacquainted with India's history and the peculiar difficulties it introduced, for in *The Fortnightly* more than a quarter of a century before, he had shown that, although there was indisputably "boundless room for improvement" in England's methods of control, nevertheless her government of India had not been an impoverishing one. Indeed, it was at that time he had declared that he had been "listening to Indian officials of all kinds . . . and reading sheafs of Indian documents" *for years* and so was "quite prepared for the most sombre view of Indian prospects." Always, however, preoccupied as he was with the idea of progress and improvement in human relations, he faced the facts of English domination in India and wondered: was it for good or for ill that Britain had imposed on herself the burden of ruling that most alien of lands? In 1909 he was "quite candid" in not knowing at all whether it was a "blessing" for either country that the "great responsibility fell upon England." After a hundred years it was significant that she still allowed no native to command a regiment (1878).

In what Morley did as Secretary for India, in the positive additions he made to the record of the conduct of Indian affairs, it must be admitted that this second chapter in his political life is superior to the first for it bore fruit immediately and tangibly. The story of his secretaryship consists of two parts: the first concerned with Morley the policeman, and the second with Morley the law-maker. Both can be outlined in brief. Early in 1907 extreme disorder broke out in India. Agitators, hostile to English rule, were inciting natives to revolt and sowing dissatisfaction among Hindu regiments. Bombs were thrown, lives were lost, widespread anarchy was imminent. Alarmed by the possibilities of rapidly aggravated dissension, Morley had the two chief spreaders of sedition captured and deported immediately, without trial. To do this he had recourse to an old law, the so-called Regulation of 1818. The riots were quelled and anarchy averted but sporadic outbursts of animosity continued, and in 1908 the rusty Regulation was again called into service to deport nine more potential subverters. Such was the disciplinary part of his activity; the legislative was more constructive. Soon after his taking of office he had announced to Parliament that he and his colleague, the Governor-General, were planning to institute reforms in Indian administration, for he was still of a mind that there was "boundless room for improvement." And true to his word, in 1906 he laid "on the anvil" a bill for certain corrections. After three years of debate, reconsideration, and reshaping, the legislation became law and the Morley-Minto Reforms inaugurated a new era for India. In four years he had succeeded in bettering the personnel of the councils for both the Secretary of State in Whitehall and the Viceroy in India by the addition to them of qualified natives (to his own he appointed a Mohammedan as well as a Hindu), and in making the various provincial legislative councils in India more truly representative by enlarging them and abolishing the hitherto invariable majority held by their "official," English-appointed members.[6]

For both the disciplinary and legislative achievements during his five years in office, Morley was unsparingly criticized. On the one hand, his stifling of subversive plotters was denounced as tyrannical licence, and on the other, his initiated reforms were viewed apprehensively as "the first step down that slippery slope at the bottom of which lies a parliamentary government for India," even though he himself had earlier said that if his act contributed "directly or necessarily" to such an end, he would have "nothing to do with it." One political critic sardonically dismissed his appointment of natives to his council as a "careful selection of nullities."

It would be easy, however, to defend his conduct in both parts. At the outset one could excuse it if it were inconsistent or unwise, by citing in his behalf his own extenuating dictum in *Studies in Conduct* more than forty years before: "It is better to hold a good theory, with occasional deflections, than a bad and cynical one, up to which one can always act in its integrity." But such excusing is not at all necessary. To all of those sensationalizing what they considered the falling-off of the old Liberal who had fought so hard for self-government for Ire-

---

[6] Morley never ceased to acknowledge that the reforms originated with Viceroy Minto. The function of the provincial councils was not altered; for the most part they remained advisory, recommending bodies, and the Viceroy's veto remained final. The new Indian "unofficial" majorities, however, were popularly elected. There were other details in the reforms, to be sure, but a discussion of them is beyond the purpose of this book. For comment on all particulars of the Bill, see E. Major, *Viscount Morley and Indian Reform* (Nisbet, March, 1910), 190 pp.

land, it could have been shown that Morley had never for a minute prescribed for Hindus or New Zealand aborigines what he had authorized for the Irish. There was no inconsistency in his policy. The most important principle he had learned from Comte almost a half century before had been that of relativity: societies exhibit varying degrees and qualities of civilization, from place to place and age to age; they must therefore be treated according to the stage of development they have reached, and no one set of recommendations can be applied as a universal solution to human difficulties. It was this conviction which had prompted him, in condemning the Zulu War in 1879, to berate the British for their stupidity in not seeing that the Zulus actually did have, although crude, a moral code and a polity, and in not realizing that it was impossible to change overnight a simple, semi-savage system of living into the complex pattern of a highly civilized nation.

Equally conspicuous and equally important in Morley's Indian administration was his allegiance to Burkean principles. Nobody who criticized him in 1909 as a Liberal apostate should have forgotten that in his historical study of Burke, his first real literary creation, in 1867, he had revealed a natural bent toward conservatism which his fondness for Burke's grand utterances on the subject served only to strengthen. The lifelong admiration for Burke, evidenced continually by quotations from his works, was inescapable and far too significant to be overlooked. Even in the most heated and shortest-tempered of his *Fortnightly* controversies he had been quick to refute charges of nihilistic sans-Culottism and explain what he, as a "most ardent" and advanced Liberal really believed; his "practical and political reason" had taught him "that the antiquity of an arrangement or a prevalent idea is no reason for assailing it, but . . . a very good reason, so far as it goes, for leaving it where it stands." Although he never approached the

extremes of Burke's reverence for the past, for Burke had super-
naturalized it, he nevertheless learned from him that

Those nations have the best chance of escaping a catastrophe . . . who find
a way of opening the most liberal career to the aspirations of the present,
without too rudely breaking with all the traditions of the past.

He shared Burke's valuation of order, too; only a year before
succeeding to the Indian secretaryship he had declared to Americans that a free community without order deserved no freedom.
What order would obtain if India were suddenly endowed with
freedom? As early as 1867 he had answered that question for
himself: no matter how noble England's motives might be, if
she withdrew from India, she would "be leaving the country
and its inhabitants to disaster and confusion far worse than
any" she had ever inflicted upon it. Not once in his career had
he even whispered Home Rule for India. How, then, could
disparagers accuse him of being a turncoat?

Although such facts, in the explanation of his administration, should have been apparent to all observers who pretended
to know him, they were, on the contrary, widely overlooked. He
himself was alert to the failure to understand his conduct and
was amused, if occasionally stung, by the misrepresentations
of it that were rife. Condemned after his deportations of sedi-
tious Hindus as a violator of the Magna Charta, a tyrant of
the stamp of Charles the First, an iron-fisted extirpator
like Strafford "or even Cromwell in his worst moments," he
laughed and rejoined that "in historical parallels" he was
"really fairly prepared." To be sure, what he had done had
amounted to a suspension of *habeas corpus*; it had been "arbitrary power" that he had wielded and he would be the first to
forswear it as a regular procedure. But after all, the circumstances had been exceptional, and if his temporary policy of
"Reason of State" was "full of mischief and full of danger,"
so was sedition. Like Burke he was willing to bear with griev-

ances until they had festered into crimes, but in criminal extremes he believed in swift recourse to decisive action. Peace and order must be maintained. If, under the conditions he had faced, the Indians had been governing themselves, their leaders would have done just as he had done—put down any attempt at insurrection with a heavy hand.[7] Besides, if anybody took the pains to investigate the plight of the deported agitators, to whom he had denied trial because he did not want them to loom as martyrs, he could find that they had been humanely treated; their detention had lasted only six or eight months, they had been subjected to no harsh treatment, their families had been carefully "looked after," and their cases had come up for periodic reconsideration by an official board of inquest. The deportation, then, had been dictated by common sense. Suppose a commandant of a fort discovered ignorant men lolling and smoking their pipes alongside powder magazines—! But if politics were after all "nothing more abstruse than good common sense," it was equally important to remember that "common sense is a kind of humanity." One had only to survey the practice of native chiefs in non-British India to see what punishment was habitually meted out for misdeeds much less objectionable than inciting revolt. And though Morley never for a moment flattered himself that Indians loved England, he did know that the more enlightened among them were thankful for her preservation of law and order, and he could cite, testifying to that, numberless telegrams which he and the Viceroy had received. The Indian leader Gokhale, for example, had declared publicly that his country had been saved from chaos, and among Indian newspapers there was at least one which did not doubt for a second that, with German or Russian overlords in

---

[7] On the subject of the justification of British government of India, Morley could quote Mill reverently: "Government by the dominant country is as legitimate as any other if it is the one which in the existing state of civilization of the subject people most facilitates their transition to our state of civilization." See *Speeches on Indian Affairs*, p. 64.

Morley's place, it would have been "a case of decapitation and not deportation" for the inflammatory nationalists. Morley himself liked to think of his whole behavior in terms of the figure with which a sympathetic journalistic colleague described it: "this swings on the tide but the anchor holds."

Like Burke and Macaulay before him, Morley held that a public man who spent much time in vindicating his consistency was making a mistake. Still, without apologizing, he could not resist pointing out from time to time, in addresses before Parliament, in speeches to his Scottish constituency, in articles for magazines, some essential facts about his relation to India. The vastness of India and the immensity of its population, its heterogeneity and its maze of minorities, its inherent mysticism, its too numerous and conflicting religions, its caste system, inconceivably gradated and intricate, its perpetual misery and discontent resulting from annual plagues (from which, mysteriously, Europeans appeared to be immune), and its growing intellectual unrest, produced and nurtured by compulsory contact with an educational curriculum of Shakespeare, Bacon, Milton, Burke, and Mill—all of these things led an administrative secretary to realize doubly the profundity in Burke's observation: "How weary a step do those take who endeavour to make out of a great mass a true political personality." What made the past government of India especially reprehensible was that it had amounted to nothing more than an alternation of moments of spasmodic concentration and energy with long hours of neglect and stagnation. Morley had determined in taking office that the time had come for translating into at least partial fulfillment the promises made earlier in the century in the two greatest steps in Anglo-Indian history since 1784: the Act of 1833, about which James Mill had said, "For the future, fitness is to be the criterion of eligibility"; and the Queen's Proclamation of 1858, in which Victoria herself had willed that Indians "so far as may be . . . of whatever race or creed, be freely and impartially admitted to offices" in the Royal service. Those words, "so far as may be," hitherto neglected, Morley would interpret henceforth "in a liberal and generous sense."

To be sure, Macaulay had been right: India in the nineteenth century was India in the fifth century, and advancing her through fourteen hundred years was "a stupendous process." With that, he concurred; but stupendous though it was, the task, in the challenge it contained, was "one of the most glorious . . . ever confided to any country." What must be ever kept in mind was the necessity for raising India slowly, stage by stage and degree by degree, to a modern utilization of her incalculable capacities. Her growth must, above all else, be gradual and regular, "in strictest measure even." Morley, who, nearly fifty years before, had realized the unfruitfulness of a philosophy of short cuts, affirmed with equal conviction that invaluable for administering India, too, were time and industry and the maintenance of a thoroughly open mind. So, averse to the label "impatient idealist," although, he admitted, there was a time when he had been one, and unsympathetic to the charge that he had been "hurried into the policy of repression," he defined his reforms as "a prudently guarded expansion of popular government," and summarized his conduct as one "of firmness, of slow reform."

Finally, in vindicating his consistency, Morley answered those critics who charged him with having usurped the authority of the Viceroy and having ruled India willfully, autocratically from Whitehall.[8] He made not the slightest pretence to disbe-

---

[8] J. H. Morgan maintains ("The Personality of Lord Morley," *Quarterly Review*, CCXLI, January, 1924) that much of the agitation in India during Morley's regime "was in a large measure directly due to a persistence continued too long and carried too far in the policy of his governing India from Whitehall." He adds that he criticized Morley in print for this but that Morley made no attempt at refutation. It is Morgan, too, who tells that Morley, sometime after his acceptance of his Viscountship, announced, "I think my fellow Peers welcome me *since they have discovered I can govern India.*" ("More Light on Lord Morley," *North American Review*, CCXXI, March, 1925.) According to J. A. Spender ("Lord Morley, Last of Victorian Liberals," *Living Age*, CCCXIX, November, 1923), Morley extended himself

lieve himself the chief instrument in the Indian government, but he was not at all a self-constituted autarch. He had adequate authority for his assumption of his position, for Victoria herself in her Proclamation of 1858 had specified that her newly created Viceroy was to be "subject to such orders and regulations as he" should "from time to time, receive through one of" her "Principal Secretaries of State," who, in turn, was to take over all powers formerly held (since 1772) by the Directors of the East India Company. Quite apart, however, from the question of the validity of Morley's assumption of supreme responsibility is the fact that inside his office in Whitehall his "tyranny" recommended itself to his colleagues and the members of his staff. Deprecating the curt, hard, "ultra-official" tone of most of the administrative correspondence, he assured his co-workers, "Benignity is not other than a virtue, even in a great public office." After long days of Cabinet or committee meetings, official conferences, and interviews, he often would urge his secretary and various subordinates to go on home and leave him to finish his tasks alone, which took him not seldom until late at night to do. But these were labors of love, and if he sometimes erred on the side of assiduity himself, he was never slow in reminding others that he did not believe in their "killing themselves with zeal."

The Indian chapter in Morley's life cannot be closed without citing one of its most talked-about occurrences, his withdrawal from the House of Commons in 1908 and entrance with a Viscountship into the House of Lords. The act was fully as unexpected and as seemingly contradictory of all Morleyan

with his first secretarial dispatch and then passed it enthusiastically across his desk with a gesture: "There! What do you think of that? Not quite so bad for the poor theorist and rhetorician!" Another friend and observer, G. P. Gooch, later said, however ("Lord Morley," *Contemporary Review,* CXXIV, November, 1923), that Morley had to be "persuaded" to employ the Regulation of 1818 in the first place and that he was so self-conscious about having done it that he wrote to his Viceroy, Minto, in India to abandon the policy of "imprisonment without charge or trial."

principle as the earlier deportations had been. Many of his adherents were thrown into consternation by the news that suddenly confronted them in the newspapers. Here was proof to confirm their worst fears that the buck had lost his horns, that democratic "Fighting John" had become a reactionary renegade, an impotent aristocrat. Was he not belatedly showing up for just what he had derided more than a generation earlier, the unstable democrat, inflated by sentimental imagination, "whose wings fall off in middle age and leave him to flop down in the House of Lords"? Even his oldest devoted friend, George Meredith, was plunged into "some turmoil" by the notice of his title, but he managed finally to conclude that it was good for both Morley "and the country." How could a man who, with professed conscientiousness, had all his life described "the institution of hereditary rank" as "the most singular" among "all ways of gratifying a democratic community," jibed incessantly at the "antics" of the House of Lords, and coined the phrase "mend them or end them" about that same body, permit himself to become identified with nobility and take his place among its exponents? Was he recanting and disavowing all his old strictures against it? Had those who worried known the circumstances surrounding the move, they would have seen that it was only a surface deviation. For a foolish consistency Morley had no more use than Emerson himself, and he refused to have one squatting like a hobgoblin in his mind. Practical considerations dictated that he protect himself. He was old, and his diminishing strength and increasing deafness compelled him to accept a seat in the upper House, where the debate was less rigorous, the tempo slower. To his constituency in Scotland he confided that he was unable any longer to represent them; he could not do justice to their claims and at the same time transact Indian affairs with the full attention they demanded. To concentrate and spare his energies for the more important task, he must move in among the leisurely Lords.[9] He had an admirable historical precedent—almost a vindication itself—for his change: in the eighteenth century, William Pitt the elder had gone over to the upper chamber, and for similar reasons.

Justified as his conduct was, however, Morley did not escape being self-conscious about it. Among his companions he almost invariably referred to his new location as "the other place" and he obstinately opposed being addressed with his new title. In the House of Lords itself he never became wholly at home, if the account of one of his associates who observed him there can be trusted.[10] He was almost pathetic to watch, creeping in stealthily "as though . . . afraid of meeting the ghost of his former self," stiff except "when his old friend the Lord Chancellor" nodded to him and called him John, shivering and looking around uneasily whenever he was addressed as the Noble Viscount, sitting immobile and detached, his face "steeled with an expression of weariness and disappointment," except when "the old lion" in him was aroused by challenging speeches on Indian affairs or his eyes were lighted up by "ironical reflection on the wastefulness of Parliamentary procedure and the insincerities of partisan politics." In the long run, however, his healthy sense of humor through the whole affair reassured his closest friends. Not long after his Viscountship, a newspaper wit celebrated it:

> When Morley said, "Let's end the Lords,
> Or, at the least, let's mend 'em,"
> We little thought what pregnant words
> Composed that vague addendum.

[9] J. A. Spender (op. cit.) has also suggested that Morley was perhaps embarrassed by being a senior in the House of Commons without being a party leader.

[10] See I. N. Ford, "John Morley in Politics," The Outlook, XC (September 26, 1908).

Today we learn how much they meant:
His Majesty, as I count,
Improves the peers by ten per cent
In making John a Viscount.

When one of his staff showed him these lines in *The Pall Mall Gazette*, he read them with relish.

His resignation of the Indian secretaryship in 1910 and his appointment that year to the Lord Presidency of the Council mark the conclusion of the second chapter in Morley's political life and the opening of the final period, the shortest and least active of the three. By this time almost a venerable figure in English politics, most of the honors being paid to him were in tribute to his past experience, or out of deference to his seniority. During 1911-1912, for example, after having received the Order of Merit in 1902 and served as minister-in-attendance on the king during a royal visit to Scotland, he was one of four chosen to administer the affairs of the realm while King George travelled in India. But there were two occasions when he assumed a larger stature and acted again with assertion and effect. In 1911, to break down their opposition to a bill which would leave them only a suspensory veto and remove entirely their jurisdiction over money matters, Morley had the satisfaction of standing before his fellow peers and assuring them that if they did not vote for the passage of the bill, he would see that the royal patents in his hand, already signed by the king for the creation of new peerages, were put into swift execution. This was one of the supreme moments in his life, one in which he felt himself most strongly the man of action, the wielder of power. The second demonstration of will came three years later in his resignation from the Cabinet over the crisis of the World War. He could see no reason for England's declaration of hostilities against Germany and he was sure that for the future the consequences of any large-scale continental struggle would be

catastrophic. He saw himself enmeshed and duped by what he
had declared as Indian Secretary he had no gift for, "artful
diplomacy." The old dream of England as the high-minded
and benignant guardian of European peace was shattered forever. Bitter and sadly resolute, he withdrew to his private life,
content there to let the rest be silence.

II

Morley's stature as a politician is not difficult to discern, and
his contribution as a statesman does not forbid appraisal. In
spite of that, however, much nonsense has been written about
him. Antipathetic moderns who dismiss him as a rhetorical but
weak stamp of Mill are no less unintelligent than sentimental
eulogists who exalt him as Honest John, a name he wincingly
disliked, and uphold his entire career as one long exhibition of
self-effacing devotion to the cause of humanity. To the end he
was attentive to fame and as suspicious as he had been in the
days of *The Saturday Review* of all self-styled "philosophers"
who contemptuously left it for fools. During the last twenty-five
years of his life he was subject to much misunderstanding at
the hands of a new generation. Sometimes it was near-abuse
through impugnment of his personal integrity, as when in 1911
he was denounced in *Blackwoods* as "a Jacobin who is always
willing to bend to the storm of popular fury" and his Indian
policy was branded in *The Spectator* as hypocritically "blended
conciliation and repression," artfully concealed in his speeches
by their wealth of "unfair imputation, of artificial antithesis,
of avoidance of issues by a turn of irony." More often it was
censure of his "outworn" political creed by hasty young Liberals of the "new" school who had not taken the pains to discover what he really stood for. In 1898 he was attacked by an
anonymous writer in *The Fortnightly* as "a cast-iron adherent
of Manchesterism," a die-hard who had not "shed the skin of

his economic adolescence," a "disintegrationist" in opposing imperialism, in short, one of the "two philosophers in the British Empire capable of learning anything and everything except the secrets of that Empire." *The Saturday Review* in 1905 labeled his attempt to rally English youth to his banner as futile and lamented his fondness for the "old watchwords" as senile; the paltriness of the writer's intelligence was betrayed, however, by his contending that to Morley political reform had always been more "than social reform, a vote . . . better than bread; pulling down lords and bishops and disestablishing churches . . . better work than protecting workmen against dangerous trades." And in 1906 an Oxford graduate, lawyer, and author who should have known better, after creditably describing Morley's temperament, went on to deplore that his Liberalism upheld "principles of unchecked individual liberty and unchecked competition," and then deprecated "its hastiness, its over-confidence in its own judgment, its scanty respect for other creeds and philosophies and methods of work, its readiness to substitute the artificial for the natural"!

If consistency is the criterion of political greatness, then Morley was among the greatest. To the last his Liberalism was faithful to the sources from which it derived. He retained his belief in the voting franchise, drawn from John Bright, and he never outgrew his loyalty to Free Trade or his anti-militarism, developed in him by his absorption in Cobden. Most important, however, in actuating him politically were the principles he had inherited from Mill and the groundwork of convictions constructed out of Burke: Mill's moral Utilitarianism, his confidence in disciplined, "ethicalized" reason, his trust in an enlightened minority, his faith in the democratic pattern as the best means for producing leaders; Burke's breadth of vision in not identifying nations with individuals ("I do not know the method of drawing up an indictment against a whole people."), his mistrust of abstract "rights,"[11] his insistence on patience and slow change, his love of order. Morley was eclectic, it is true; he originated nothing. But he was eclectic in the highest sense; after assimilating ideas, he gave them living force and was an inspiring embodiment of them.

If prescience be the sole determinant of political rank, Morley must again be assigned to a station not far from the top. He always marvelled at Burke's "feat of sagacity" in predicting, a decade or so before it arrived, the dictatorship of Napoleon. In the light of what happened in 1940, was his own prediction so much less extraordinary—his prophetic warning, uttered in 1867, that, if strife between France and Germany was not extinguished, Germany would one day achieve a "monstrous pacification" by overrunning Belgium and the Netherlands as well as France? To be sure, prognostication was not his forte and he laid no claim to the role of prophet, but, unfortunately, many things have been forgotten by dissenters who deny that he had any vision for the signs of the times. He was so outraged by England's treacherous seizure of the Transvaal in 1877, on the pretext that the Dutch were a troubled, unselfsufficient society and needed protection, that he declared an eventual German absorption of Czechoslovakia on the same grounds, a betrayal no more incredible and no more criminal! If he could not foretell with certainty the duration of it, at least he recognized sadly in 1880 that civilization was entering "a great armed period, an era of violence and the sword." Although, with regard to the African wars of the last fifteen years of the century, his pronouncement of 1879 was somewhat premature, that in the future a prime minister could wage a long

[11] In 1867 in *Edmund Burke* Morley wrote that no figment of metaphysics "is more monstrous than this of the final and absolute existence of a Right. As if Right in the highest sense of all were something beyond a test, and, still more absurd and mischievous, as if any given right were possessed of qualities beyond those of a measurable, fluctuating, and conventional value, assigned to it by its greater or less conformity with the conditions of the general convenience."

war only if the English people were convinced that "the very independence of the country" was in danger, it is being borne out dramatically in 1942 by Winston Churchill and his nation. Equally far-sighted was his conviction that England would never enjoy the fruits of a high-minded peace through a pitiful isolation from the affairs of the continent. Was the "Versailles armistice" (1918-1939) after all only the first for England in that series of armed truces which he decreed would be the lot of western Europe if England persisted in refraining from using her potentially great moral power to conciliate continental antagonists and point the way actively to peace?

It is true that Morley's reading of the Book of Empire for the future was only half true; he was right in 1884 when he maintained that England's colonies would oppose "artificial centralization" and that they would increasingly desire "expansion . . . along lines and in channels which they may spontaneously cut out for themselves," but he was wide of the mark, if the War of 1914 is any evidence, when he stated that close imperial co-operation in the event of war was unbelievable, for who could imagine Australian legislatures reconciling "their constituents at the other side of the globe to paying money for a war, say, for the defence of Afghanistan against Russia, or for the defence of Belgian neutrality"! He erred, too, in believing so wholeheartedly in the advantages of representative government as to maintain that for any western European nation, it would, among other things, arbitrarily increase "the state of national self-respect" to the point where it would become a protection against "unreasonable jealousy of other nations." The experience of Germany after 1918 under the Weimar Republic, of course, offers all-too-unhappy proof to the contrary. Curiously, his faith in Germany blinded him to the menacing growth in the twenty-five years before 1914 of militant, autocratic ultra-Germanism and he dismissed the doctrines of Heinrich Treitschke, one of its foremost inculcators, as "twenty times as little tending to edification" as Machiavelli.[12]

Finally, as specimens of Morley's prescience, are his statements about labor and industry. "The wisest statesman," he had written in *The Fortnightly* in 1877, "—unless he is over sixty—is he who keeps his mind most on the alert for new economic forms." Measured by his own definition, he does not appear very farsighted in his unrelenting condemnation of the Eight Hours Bill in 1895 as an infringement upon workers' rights. But he was clear-visioned in foreseeing that sooner or later a "great economic revolution would convulse the earth" and that the great problem confronting every country was, therefore, to devise the best kind of industrial organization for withstanding it. If capitalism for western civilization is doomed, if Socialism is inevitable, then Morley's resolute stand against the Socialists (against the abolition of private property, the state appropriation of capital, and the equal distribution of products) and his firm belief in a modified, enlightened capitalism as the solution for England must be acknowledged inadequate. It may always be questioned, nevertheless, whether the humane capitalism which he advocated, with workers and employers both guided by "moral and social motives," has ever been tried, and whether his verdict on Socialism is not true—that under such a system, human stupidity, apathy, sloth, and brutishness will be just as likely to "continue to strew the way with wastrels and wrecks."

Actually what defines Morley's place in political history is neither consistency nor prescience. It is capacity for leadership; and in that, after a quarter of a century, he shows up strikingly

[12] In a lecture on democracy at the University of Manchester on June 28, 1912. "No Professor in this University could keep a class for a month upon Politik of that stamp." (See Sirdar Ali Khan, *The Life of Lord Morley*, p. 323.) It has been pointed out elsewhere how ironic was his failure to estimate German forces, in the face of his youthful acumen for revealing in his French studies the cataclysmic, though slow, growth in France more than a hundred years earlier of the ideas sown by the pre-Revolutionary philosophers.

deficient. More things than one testify to the shortcoming. In the first place, he did not possess the irresistible assurance about himself which a successful politician, to lead others, needs in abundance. He never transmitted driving conviction, never compelled people through the contagion of his own enthusiasm, to follow him. He was prey to doubts about himself and nocturnal misgivings about his offices and policies. Time after time in dejection he drafted and mailed letters of resignation, which were invariably consigned by his superiors to the fire; "how many burnt offerings" they had made, according to an intimate friend, not even Prime Minister Asquith could tell. Moreover, he was not a powerful, commanding speaker. In Parliament, after a stumbling failure in his maiden speech, he managed to recover and become an effective "solo performer" in carefully prepared addresses, but he never mastered the spontaneous give-and-take of debate. In Asquith's words, he was always "oppressed by the difficulty of satisfying his literary conscience in impromptu speech." Outside, on the lecture platform, though through perseverance he gained a certain competency of delivery, enough to make him one of the most reputable speakers between 1887 and 1900, the influence he exerted was through his transparent conviction, and, in later years, through his "awkward gestures," "husky voice," and "ragged sentences." He impressed listeners and won sympathy, but he never excited, never impelled.

Nothing, however, more tellingly reveals his inability to lead than his conduct during the outbreak of the first World War. Leadership means making others do and follow, and that by nature he did not have. A general must generate. His decision to resign from the Cabinet rather than violate his principles was lofty and laudable. But it was only a subdued, departing gesture of the hand where a bold, challenging sweep of the arm was needed. Why did he not speak in Parliament condemning what he knew to be the growing intention of his colleagues to declare war? Why did he not make at least one attempt to stem the tide by exposing before the assembled Houses some of the ministerial duplicity he had discovered, and so prompt an investigation? To be sure, he was old and weakened, but what a cause he had to plead, and what a moment it would have been! What a seizure Burke—or Gladstone—would have made of the opportunity! Why, at least, did he not take the offensive and wrestle with his Cabinet associates to dissuade them from their purpose? The whole story of his resignation, with its sequel of the years of silence and the posthumous appearance of his own self-vindication, shows him too prone to desist from further effort, once he had satisfied his own conscience by acting according to his convictions.[13] Setting an example, indispensable as it is in political leadership, is not enough; other men must be prevailed upon and drawn to imitate it. The withdrawal from the Cabinet thus remains a fitting final gesture in his public life; it was at once the consummation of his career and the supreme revelation of its deficiency.

Men of action, Morley always held, must be judged by the

[13] The posthumous self-vindication is, of course, Morley's *Memorandum on Resignation*, composed in August, 1914, and published by Macmillan's in 1928. J. H. Morgan says that he urged Morley in 1922 to make public the *Memorandum*, but in vain. Moreover, according to Morgan, Morley's strenuousness in trying to free himself of complicity in the diplomacy that resulted in England's entrance into the war was foredoomed. Condemn Lord Grey as he would, he should have scented the outcome of the government's foreign policy, since he himself had been, from at least 1910, a member of the Committee for Imperial Defense. The fact is, says Morgan, that in his old age his memory failed and he would forget such important occurrences as that in 1910 he had been present at a meeting of the British and French General Staffs and had written in some agitation on the outside of an envelope containing certain military plans, "Doubtful if I ought to approve of this. But I suppose it's in the interests of European peace." See, for remarks about Morley and the war, Morgan's two articles, "The Personality of Lord Morley," Parts I and II, *Quarterly Review*, CCXLI (January and April, 1924), and "More Light on Lord Morley," *North American Review*, CCXXI (March, 1925).

R. Beazley ("John Morley and the War," *The Nation*, CXXVIII, March, 1929) calls Morley's long post-war silence an "unheroic self-effacement" and says that in 1917 he was asked by Lord Lansdowne to co-operate in leading a movement to end the war, his co-operation to mean, among other things, a publishing of his *Memorandum*, but that "through lack of courage, like the poor and timid Pope in Dante, he made the great refusal."

standards of men of action; yet his own achievement, measured alongside that of such leaders as Walpole, Pitt, and Gladstone, is third rate at best. And he had held at twenty-five, a second-rate politician poorer than a second-rate writer! What he remains admirable and memorable for is his insistence on humanity and morality in politics, his own personal adherence to high ideals. The character of Lord Morley's power, as has been said, was the power of Lord Morley's character. He demonstrates, with his fortitude, his independence, his healthy disbelief in panaceas, and his conviction that legislating must be done with a view to human nature rather than an eye for a system, what the best kind of Liberalism, the Liberalism that is the liberating "fruit of education and thought" and not the "half accidental" creed of a transitory political party, can effect in an individual life.

CHAPTER FOUR

The Man of Letters (1867-1903)
Applying the Historical Method to Criticism

WHEN an obscure magazine commentator once remarked, "The critic is, we take it, the irreducible personage in John Morley's make-up," he expressed, somewhat uncouthly, the most significant fact about Morley's mind. That it was nothing if not critical is evidenced by his literary output, from first to last. Although he never formulated in an essay an exposition of his critical principles, he did harbor a set of them as fully worked out as those of Matthew Arnold; and the comprehensiveness, the vigor, and the contemporary influence of his own writing are obverse proof of what he once decreed in *The Fortnightly*: "Criticism without a doctrine can never be adequate or decisive." Not that with a doctrine, he ever became a doctrinaire, but simply that he had no more respect than Samuel Johnson for men whose attitude toward life embraced "nothing more shaped and incorporate than a little group of potential and partially incoherent tendencies."

Among his earliest printed remarks about literary criticism are his conviction in *Studies in Conduct* that a critic should have an "eye for perfection" as well as the "keenest vision for a flaw" and his contention in *Modern Characteristics* that demonstrating the beauty or truth in a work is more important than showing how it came to be written. The French critics, Sainte-Beuve, Joubert, and Villemain, he held to be excessive in the amount of personal knowledge they sought of a writer before judging his books. Nevertheless, from Sainte-Beuve's greater dispassionateness, attention to social background, and respect for heredity and physiology in moulding character, he learned not little. In 1878 he stated authoritatively in *Diderot* that, "in criticism in its literary sense," France had always been, and was still, without a rival. At the same time his familiarity with German thought constrained him to point out that in "historic criticism," more profound, Germany was supreme.

The thoroughness of Morley's doctrine is illustrated by his clear conceptions of the stuff with which he was to work, the result at which he would aim, and the method he would pursue. The critic's material was literature, which he understood at twenty-eight to be "at once the noblest result and the finest gratification of man's curiosity about his own nature and his own lot"; so conceived, it widened the range of human ideas and enriched spiritual existence. Later, with closer attention to its effects, he characterized it as "the master organon for giving men the two precious qualities of breadth of interest and balance of judgment; multiplicity of sympathies and steadiness of sight." The ultimate purpose of criticism was social. Never allowing his craft to degenerate into "an industriously compiled catalogue of notions and opinions" or "a trick of forced and artful illustration," the critic must "help to create a literary atmosphere" which would "spread a disposition for positive thought and . . . distribute knowledge." In such a function, his work, though "in superficial appearance merely an appreciation of the production of others," would be "in fact tantamount to constructive production of a really original kind," for it would help ordinary men and women to shape a coherent philosophical attitude toward life and stimulate creative writers in their search for themes. Essentially disinterested, it would derive from one who, though active in his own time, was unabsorbed by its problems and uncontaminated by its strife. Intellectual detachment, in a word, was the critic's indispensable armor. Only equipped with it could he follow the requisite method—discern the relations between a man's thought and the leading ideas of his age, then trace its connection with the intellectual climate of modern times. This method Morley described alternately as dynamic, synthetic.

In such a doctrine there was naturally little place for tenuous problems of aesthetics. A piece of poetry, for example, interested Morley either because of its relation to other poetical works, to questions of language, to matters of form, or because of its bearing on conduct and life, but not at all because of the mystery of what *per se* it was. And so the age-old controversy of literary critics over the nature of Aristotle's catharsis wearied him; there was "no subject in literature, not even the interpretation of the Apocalypse," that had "given birth to such pedantic, dismal, and futile discussion."

Morley's contributions to literature, in which his doctrine can be seen in operation, comprise a series of French studies ranging in size from monographs to full-volume biographical treatments, a single volume, *On Compromise*, in the tradition of Mill, biographies of five English political figures, and a series of essays in literary criticism.

THE FRENCH STUDIES

The French studies, extending over a period of ten years, were Morley's largest literary enterprise. He loved "the great spirits of the eighteenth century" because they had striven for progress through enlightenment, employing their broad minds to destroy prejudice, superstition, and fanaticism, to shatter the tyranny of church and state. Aware of the connection between that movement and the struggle in England in his own day, he was fired to enlist as one of the champions in the tradition of Voltaire and Diderot, helping to point the way out of darkness. Dangerous as it was in England in 1867 to undertake to interpret the French Revolution, he would dispel the prevalent ignorance and hostility regarding it by exposing for the first time both its constructive and destructive sides. Burke, in assailing its leaders in 1795, had set the tone for all subsequent English criticism; Carlyle, following, had, with an enrichment of literature, done an injustice to history. Yet in his attempt to erect a bridge of understanding across a flood of intolerance, Morley was often denounced by bigots who saw him as a subverter of English institutions. His patience was under constant trial in reminding them that "an entirely heterogeneous set of circumstances" in nineteenth-century England made a duplication of French Revolutionary procedure impossible, and in riddling their bad logic by showing that "only on the principle that who drives fat oxen must himself be fat, can it be held that who writes on Danton must be himself in all circumstances a Dantonist."

Interesting now in these controversial studies is the Maccabean ardency of their tone and the frequency with which Morley, in pointing out parallel situations between the Encyclopedists' day and his own, delivers judgment on issues hot for him in the 1870's. The smallest studies in the series are for the most part the earliest: yet, although *De Maistre* (1868), *Condorcet* (1870), *Turgot* (1871), *Vauvenargues* (1872), and *Robespierre* (1876) are brief, they are compact, direct, and so strongly written as to leave unmistakable impressions of the figures they explain.

Nobody should read the French studies, however, without consulting beforehand the last eighty-five pages of *Edmund Burke*, Morley's first volume published in his own name (1867) and undoubtedly, inadequate though he afterwards considered it, one of the few of his works most likely to survive. Evaluating the French Revolution with extraordinary perspective and comprehensiveness, these pages transmit his definitive opinions on the event and form a preface to the various studies which followed.

The Revolution broke out in France instead of elsewhere, he explains, not because social conditions were so disproportionately worse there, but because the permeation of radical political ideas had been wider and deeper. Even Louis XVI, affected by the atmosphere, had talked reform and mistakenly exhibited an "ostentatious deference to public opinion." Although it is lamentable that because of human nature, political and social changes cannot "be consummated with the same autumnal stillness and silence in which Nature works her transformations," for the suffering of men and women is indeed deplorable, yet suffering is not all that a war discloses:

> Every mass of men in volcanic moments, like the mythic Aetna, covers a Titan: and it is by the Titan only that they can be moved. It is an evil, but not an unmixed evil, that this should be so. These violent rebellions against a spiritual or social destiny too hard to be longer endured, disclose heights of sacrifice and energy and aspiration in man, a tidal sweep and depth of moral force, which progress could ill afford to spare.

There were after all certain positive results of the Revolution. It had "impregnated the political atmosphere with ethical ingredients," implanted in the forefront of politicians' minds a realization of justice "as the radical condition of all social arrangements," and renovated "the generous and sublime sentiment of the brotherhood of men," which for centuries had been lost to Christianity. Even some of its strongest opponents, like De Maistre in philosophy and Chateaubriand in religion, had "caught a measure of brightness and largeness from their adversary."

On the other hand, innumerable shortcomings and harmful effects marred the work of the Revolutionists. Tragically handicapped at the outset by a lack of practical experience, they were unable to realize the necessity in political reform "of temporizing, of compromise, of aiming not too high, of conciliating masses of opposing interest"; they were blind to the fact that France was sure, in experimenting as she was, "to call down the fierce hostility of all the other unrevolutionized governments";[1] overtaken by timorousness, they were led on from uncertainty to fear, to cruelty, whereas had they had the practice of free men in a representative government they would never have fallen into their ghastly excesses; and finally, they had failed to discern that indissoluble hostility among the nobles, the clergy, and the third estate rendered their co-operation impossible. Theorizers too abrupt in referring all problems to metaphysical principles, visionaries actuated by too much love of geometrical symmetry, they had made a fetich of Equality, whereas they should have discarded their imaginary "social contract" and preached "general utility," abandoned the dogma of "inherent right" in favor of the criterion of "general happiness." Their uprooting break with the past was to be condemned, for "those who detest the past with indiscriminate execration are sure, in the long run, to come to distrust the future also." Nevertheless their great spirit must be considered along with their visible failures. And in future decades, when perspective is clearer and indignation cooled, it will be apparent that the atrocities and anarchy of the last ten years of the eighteenth century, which loom so large because they were precipitated all at once instead of gradually, "were less, not greater" than the crimes and confusion prevalent in France since the Regency.

DE MAISTRE

Although nothing in De Maistre's ideas was tolerable to Morley, the sum of them, in opposition to the temper of the Encyclopedists, made for a startling contrast, whose dramatic value he was quick to see. He could make a clear exposition of De Maistre's theological absolutism without subscribing to it

---

[1] "It would be fairer, as it seems to me, to attribute the disastrous failure of the Revolution in France not so much to her unfitness for liberty, as to the still more imperfect preparation of her neighbors. It was the enmity of the retrograde powers of Europe which first drove her into the excesses natural to panic, and then by their flagitious designs aroused that military temper, which eventually slew her new-born freedom." (p. 231.)

himself. As a matter of fact, fairly to exhibit both answers to the question of the reconstruction of society, he had to set down the case for the reactionaries. Furthermore, proud of his broad-mindedness, he was more than a little attracted by the problem of estimating a character so antagonistic to his own.

De Maistre, intent on "absolutely killing the spirit of the eighteenth century," considered the Revolution the breakdown of French civilization, analogous to the earlier crumbling of the Roman Empire, and denounced the whole school of rationalists and Encyclopedists for having caused it. Christianity alone could restore order, and the Pope alone must be the spiritual and temporal authority controlling civilization. Councils were futile for government, since "what is doubtful for forty men is doubtful for the whole human race." Out of his arguments, however, the light of rationalism bleaches weaknesses. His God looms as only "a colossal Septembriseur, enthroned high in the peaceful heavens, demanding ever-renewed holocausts in the name of the public safety," and his contention that Christian rulers had all lived longer than non-believers and distinguishingly died of nameless illnesses is absurd. His solution, in short, each passing decade only shows more "desperate and impossible." In spite of its power to console spiritually and guide ethically, the record of the Catholic Church "as the sworn enemy of mental freedom and growth" nullifies its pretensions to renovate society. Christianity, to be restored, would have to be in an almost unrecognizably different form, with no possibility of a union between it and the temporal power. "The free church in the free state" must prevail in the future, for "if the Church has the uppermost hand, it impairs freedom; if the state is supreme, it impairs spirituality."

And with this pronouncement the essay closes. But the little work is more than just a rational penetration of Catholic politics; De Maistre as a human being interested Morley, and the first section shows him as a refugee against the background of the Revolution, with quotations from his letters to enliven the picture.

CONDORCET

Condorcet is praiseworthy for his interest in humane legal reforms, his advocacy of female emancipation, and his rare perception in holding what approached a scientific conception of history. But his optimism had led him to proclaim erroneously: "The history of the human species as a whole may be regarded as the unravelling of a hidden plan of nature for accomplishing a perfect state of civil constitution for society." In the positive scheme of things, final intentions do not exist. Admirable, too, as he is for his contributions "to the stock of science and social speculation," for his lofty sentiments, his "noble solicitude for human well-being, his eager and resolute belief in its indefinite expansion, and the devotion that sealed his faith by a destiny as tragical as any" that occurred in those bloody days, there is this vital shortcoming to face in his philosophy—"He measures only the contributions made by nations and eras to what we know; leaving out of sight their failures and successes in the elevation of moral standards and ideals, and in the purification of human passions."

TURGOT

As with Condorcet and De Maistre, so with Turgot, Vauvenargues, Robespierre. Each one, as Morley treated him, exhibited some trait of character or some accomplishment which helped to raise the Englishman's image of the Revolutionary period into bolder relief and to throw certain corner details of it, never before exposed, into clear light. Turgot, the economist so admired by Mill and revealed by him to Morley, was significant because his brief tenure as Comptroller-General at the court of Louis XVI had exposed the truth that anarchy and not despotism in the royal government was precipitating a revolution. In his earlier experience, too, as Intendant of the Generality of Limoges, he had shown himself liberal, clinging to good government as to a religion and believing in progress as well, even though, benevolently undemocratic, he had always proceeded on the grounds of "everything for the people; nothing by the people." Justice had been his watchword; it alone, and not pity or charity, could "keep the balance true among all rights and all interests." This insistence of his related him to Burke.

Attracting Morley's special admiration was Turgot's enlightened historic conception; early in life he had reached the conclusion that "all epochs are fastened together by a sequence of causes and effects; linking the condition of the world to all the conditions that have gone before it." Making him additionally congenial were his conscientious objection to Christianity and his honesty in leaving the Church, for which he had been preparing to take orders; his discernment that "it is not error that opposes the progress of truth; it is indolence, obstinacy, the spirit of routine, everything that favours inaction"; and his concern over the relative importance of the man of action and the man of letters. In common with his age, however, Turgot had fallaciously held ideas superior to morals in aiding the movement of civilization, unable, as Morley could, to look at Christianity in unbiased perspective and see that the antireligious heat of the eighteenth century had blinded materialists to benefits bequeathed by the Church to the past. The saint does have his place in history even though Turgot and his fellows "passionately threw him out from their calendar as the wooden idol of superstition," and "the leading of souls to do what is right and humane, is always more urgent than mere instruction of the intelligence as to what exactly is the right and humane."

VAUVENARGUES

Vauvenargues, in no way the philosophic equal of De Maistre or Turgot, was nevertheless, for certain of his traits, warmly likable. Despite disillusionment by early experience in the army, he had fallen into no despondency but continued to hold an equable, middle path, avoiding alike the cynicism of La Rochefoucauld and the pessimism of Pascal. Although he had moved in frivolous circles, he had never played smart in his conduct with women. He had cherished what he called "virtuous instinct" in human nature, and that Morley identified sympathetically with the reasoned prejudice in which he, like Burke, had come to place so much faith. Vauvenargues had written graceful *caractères*, too, but much more memorable are his maxims, "nearly always moderate and persuasive" and marked by "delicacy and half-reserved tenderness." To these, Morley developed a life-long attachment, using again and again several favorites in his speaking and writing.[2]

ROBESPIERRE

Robespierre, the most vivid, most animated study of the series, suggests Carlyle. Although syntactically it has nothing in common with *The French Revolution*, it nevertheless possesses something of its graphic quality and its quickness. The only picture Morley ever attempted of the Revolution at work, it succeeds in imparting movement to events between 1791 and 1794. With fine concentration characters are sketched in and

---

2 "Great truths come from the heart," "It is a great sign of mediocrity always to praise moderately," and "To carry through great undertakings, one must act as though one would never die." In an address on aphorisms in Edinburgh in 1887 Morley expressed himself thus: "Aphorism or maxim, let us remember that this wisdom of life is the true salt of literature; that those books, at least in prose, are most nourishing that are most richly stored with it; and that it is one of the main objects, apart from the mere acquisition of knowledge, which men ought to seek in the reading of books."

an atmosphere of tension is recreated. But political definition
and an analysis of the philosophical changes involved are kept
superior to the drama of the upheaval, and this separates Morley's method from Carlyle's. The expected rationalist arraignment of the Catholic Church occurs. But Robespierre is judged
and found wanting, too; incapable of vision and devoid of any
"social conception," he was only a democratic doctrinaire with
an "intrepid logic." His Feast of the Supreme Being is ridi-
culed: how could men in a complex modern society have re-
verted to the placid simplicities of a pastoral life—or adored
the outer world when they had already learned it to be only a
vast collection of phenomena obeying fixed laws? Perhaps the
chief value of the piece, however, lies in its vivid expression, of
which this single paragraph is a good specimen:

> Robespierre's style had no richness either of feeling or of phrase; no
> fervid originality, no happy violences. If we turn from a page of Rousseau
> to a page of Robespierre, we feel that the disciple had none of the sonorous
> thrill of the master; the ardour has become metallic; the long-drawn plan-
> gency is parodied by shrill notes of splenetic complaint. . . . The absence of
> these intenser qualities did not make Robespierre's speeches less effective
> for their own purpose. On the contrary, when the air has become torrid,
> and passionate utterance is cheap, then severity in form is very likely to
> pass for sense in substance. That Robespierre had decent fluency, copious-
> ness, and finish need hardly be said. . . . Robespierre was as solicitous
> about the correctness of his speech as he was about the neatness of his
> clothes; he no more grudged the pains given to the polishing of his dis-
> courses than he grudged the time given every day to the powdering of his
> hair.

VOLTAIRE

Sometime early in the first week of June 1871 Morley was
"seized, after the manner of poets, with a phrenetic and wholly
invincible oestrus—to write a monograph—Voltaire." Everything else had disappeared from his mind, he told Harrison in
a note; night and day he was possessed and stuck to his table
like a slave. "What a subject! It will be about the size of Burke

or a little bigger." His enthusiasm was justified. The single volume he produced, one of his best for quickness of intellect, liveliness of tone, and sustained interest, is mature confirmation of what, four years earlier, he had forecast in *The Fortnightly*, "that the time for understanding Voltaire is at least approaching."

The book is not an attempt to recreate eighteenth-century France or to depict Voltaire as a leading personage in the splendid artificiality of the age; the biological man is subordinated to the thinker and his career as a crusher of infamy. One meets anecdotes and quotations from letters as well as sketches of human relationships, but only those indispensable to the delineation of Voltaire the spreader of enlightenment. Moral aspects, too, as well as physical, give way to intellectual. Not that moral considerations are neglected—"there ought to be little condonation of the foibles and none at all of the moral obliquities of the dead, because this would mean the demoralization of the living"—but that they will be subordinated to "that other kind of criticism which dwells less on the final balance of good and evil than on the first innate conditions of temperament, the fixed limitations of opportunity, and the complex interplay of the two with that character, which is first their creature, and then their master." Such is Morley's scientific credo, in keeping with the tendency of the times toward more accurate and dispassionate observation. He always retained, and justly, an aversion to "the bald division of men into sheep and goats." Accordingly, the Voltaire whom he presents transcends Carlyle's *persifleur*, whose love of truth was only a "prudent calculation" and who saw history as only a tedious, endless "debating-club dispute . . . between the Encyclopédie and the Sorbonne."

Materialistic skepticism in France during Voltaire's youth, his own inclination to it, his strengthening absorption of it during his stay in England, his abhorrence of church tyranny and

social injustice, his devotion to the cause of truth and enlightenment through the great part of his life—of all of these Morley gives a clear account. True to his word, he pays as much
attention to the maturing of Voltaire's mind, to the influences
on it, as he does to its activity, once fully developed. But the
origin of such a mind baffles him. Voltaire is one of those superior spirits which loom up suddenly, anomalies in the universe of thought no less startling than sports in the animal
world. No more than science can explain biological mutations,
can history explain "the law by which the most striking varia-
tions in intellectual and spiritual quality within the human
order have had their origin." Still, despite the hopelessness of
an answer, humanity owes a debt to Voltaire. He was a miracle,
the result of "an unknown element at the bottom of the varieties
of creation, whether we agree to call that element a volition of
a supernatural being, or an undiscovered set of facts in em-
bryology."

With appropriate disinterestedness, Morley commends Voltaire for his breadth of vision in perceiving "that we must still
wait three or four hundred years" for the consummation of the
revolution in men's minds, but finds him wanting in a comprehension of the reliable, scientific sources to which a writer must
go for an understanding of a society; Voltaire was too inclined
to depend on gossip, reminiscences, and diaries instead of in-
vestigating, and coming to grips with, problems of finance,
trade, agricultural production. So, too, although he had dis-
criminated carefully between ecclesiastical dogma and the
Christianity of the Sermon on the Mount, to whose humanity
"not a man then alive" was "more keenly sensible," yet he had
been historically short-sighted in not admitting the nurturing
by the Catholic Church of the groping, inchoate civilization of
the Middle Ages. Still his fight against church hypocrisy and
superstition had been open, bold, relentless, flashing, not at all
like the campaign of the nineteenth century, full of

. . . cowardice of heart and understanding, when each controversial man at arms is eager to have it thought that he wears the colors of the other side, when the theologian would fain pass for rationalist, and the free-thinker for a person with his own orthodoxies, if you only knew them, and when philosophic candour and intelligence are supposed to have hit their final climax in the doctrine that everything is both true and false at the same time.

Early in his *Fortnightly* criticism Morley had decried the fact that "in popular speech morality and immorality" were "most absurdly confined to transactions with a woman in them." "Moral hypochondriacs" were intolerable in forever confusing art with morality; Doré's illustrations for Tennyson's "Elaine" could no more be considered moral or immoral than could gravitation. Nevertheless, Voltaire's *La Pucelle* incites him to question the justifiability of sexual licentiousness as an enhancement in narrative. That Condorcet, admirable in almost every respect, had defended the ribald account of Joan makes it no easy thing to condemn. In indicting it, he refers to the basic postulates of his conception of human morals. Literature as an interpretation of life must help to make it effectual, to give it unity; and unity of life is dependent on the integrity of human relations. "Our identity does by no means consist in a historic continuity of tissues, but in an organic moral coherency of relation," and, in the absence of any divine ordinance, "it is this, which alone, if we consider the passing shortness of our days, makes life a whole, instead of a parcel of thrums, bound together by an accident." In the face of such a sound and dignified averment *La Pucelle* shrinks pitiably; its shameless, sportive promiscuity sentences it, for "is not every incentive and every concession to vagrant appetite a force that enwraps a man in gratification of self, and severs him from duty to others, and so a force of dissolution and dispersion?" Thus Morley vindicates himself, corrects Condorcet, and passes criticism on Voltaire, but dispassionately he reminds his readers of

Candide's own remark: "The unwise value every word in an author of repute." His last reflections on the matter explain the scurrilous treatment of the virgin-martyr not by an innately immoral Voltaire, but by two features of his age: its licentiousness, grown out of the glossed sensuality of the royal court, and its contempt for the medieval valuation of purity, a natural but regrettable accompaniment of the breakdown of church dogma.

Morley rightly places Voltaire below the greatest masters of literature, because of his lack of spiritual profundity and imaginative power. Only in that kind of literature which is "to diffuse the light by which common men are able to see the great host of ideas and facts that do not shine in the brightness of their own atmosphere," do Voltaire's curiosity, intelligence, frankness, wit, and marvelous facility of expression make him unrivalled. Even in comedy, "the veritable comedy of human character and life," he falls short of highest achievement. In caricature he "has no equal" and in *Candide* or *Zadig*, for example, he has risen as high as wit can go, but his imaginative inability to identify himself with a wide variety of lives outside his own, his lack of a "tragic breadth" of view and of a wide "consciousness of contrasts" mark him inferior to "Shakespeare, Moliere, and even Aristophanes."

Over the perfect appropriateness of Voltaire's prose as a vehicle for his ideas—its lucidity, it flexibility, its economy, "where the nimbleness of the sentence is in proportion to the firmness of the thought"—Morley cannot resist exclaiming. No more able to tolerate strange manners and uncouth attire in writing than in clothing, he praises Voltaire for abstaining from "bastard attempts to reproduce in words deep and complex effects which can only be adequately presented in colour or in the combination of musical sounds." Nothing was more repugnant to his orthodoxy than the literary *enfant terrible*. Whitman's exploits in bold free verse he held beneath consideration, and many of the experiments of French poets in "art

for art's sake" became anathema to him. Words without sense
he dismissed as "the smirks and affectations of mere elegant
dispersiveness."

Excellent though Voltaire's own style had been, to it could
be traced a decline in "the purity and harmony" of prose in
both England and France. His own "reaction against a spurious dignity of style," lost proportion and direction in the hands
of imitators who, without his reason and balance, identified
spurious dignity with real dignity and blindly attacked all the
intellectual and aesthetic elements of the old order. This was
to be deplored: "an assumed vulgarity tries to pass for native
homeliness, and, as though a giant were more impressive for
having a humped back, some men of genius seem only to make
sure of fame by straining themselves into grotesqueness." Academic rule, after all, has its place, and painstakingness cannot
fail to have an "exceedingly great reward."

Obviously Morley did not consider himself Voltaire's suc-
cessor. Harrison told him in 1873 that, although his prose was
potentially better than that of anybody else except George
Eliot, it was still "not yet at its best by reason of its excessive
richness and audacity and complexity." Calling him "a prose
Browning who delights the cultured but who is too difficult for
the multitude," he urged him to "speak to the people in words
of Cobbett-like simplicity." That Morley realized the character
of his prose is evident in *Voltaire*. It was not that he did not aim
at simplicity, but that the sort of simplicity in which Voltaire
had excelled was no longer possible; the closest thing to it was
"an intensely elaborated kind." Society had become more complex, knowledge had expanded and branched immeasurably,
with the result that Truth had to be followed "slowly along
paths steep and devious"; "hence, as all good writers aim at
simplicity and directness," there had grown "a new style, in
which the rays of many side-lights are concentrated in some
single phrase." Style always remained for Morley a reflection

of habits of mind, and of them "the spirit of science and fact and ordered knowledge" continued to be the shaper. Looking back years later, in 1911, he was to see that a whole new vocabulary dated from 1859; science had ushered in an "epoch of quieter style after the giants: Carlyle, Ruskin, and Macaulay."[3]

But his own style in 1871 was characterized by more than an "intensely elaborated" simplicity. "Every man is born with all the centuries in him," he used to remind his readers, and certainly when he wrote *Voltaire* he had much in him of the seventeenth and eighteenth centuries which found expression in marked stylistic tendencies. Of the clarity, the balance, the sententiousness of eighteenth-century prose the work has such representatives as, "His [Voltaire's] was one of the robust and incisive constitutions, to which doubt figures as a sickness, and where intellectual apprehension is an impossibility," and "Where it is a duty to worship the sun, it is pretty sure to be a crime to examine the laws of heat." Offsetting this epigrammatic keenness is much that reveals an affinity for seventeenth-century unction. From the impassioned peroration of the book comes this line:

And a man will be already in no mean paradise, if at the hour of sunset a good hope can fall upon him like harmonies of music that the earth shall still be fair and the happiness of every feeling creature still receive a constant augmentation and each cause yet find worthy defenders, when the memory of his own poor name and personality has long been blotted out of the brief recollection of men for ever.

Frequent, too, are figures drawn on classical models, like that of Voltaire's conception of Truth—"a goddess . . . to be sought in the free tumult and joyous strife of many voices, there vindicating her own majesty and marking her own children"—and figures deriving from the Bible, like that in the question which, defending Voltaire's destructive criticism, asks, "Has Jericho

---

[3] See "Words and Their Glory," *Politics and History*, pp. 197-210.

always fallen without the blasts from the seven trumpets?" The long line, the sonority, the majesty of great seventeenth-century prose had much power over Morley, and he had read the chief divines with profit.

Forty years after *Voltaire*, he was to tell an annual General Meeting of the English Association that the age of grandeur had died with Burke and that it is only natural that prose should be unemotional "where the themes and issues are those of scientific truth." He was apparently forgetting that in his *Fortnightly* days he, too, had been a man of "supreme issues, earnest convictions, eager desire to convert and persuade," and that these things which "moved to eloquence at its highest" had not at all ceased to exist after Sir Thomas Browne, Raleigh, Bacon, Hooker, Burke. In this address there is something almost apologetic about his explanation of the change in the tone of prose—something apologetic and close to a palliation of his conscience, too, so far as his earlier work is concerned. Aware that his own books, although not forgotten, have certainly not survived on the crest of the wave like those of the "classic masters," remembering the great career as historian prophesied for him by Harrison and Meredith years before, recalling regrets like that expressed by Hardy over the wasting of himself by an entrance into politics, is he not attempting to extenuate his failure to establish his place among the most eloquent? And when he confesses, "If we are on our way to a quieter style, I am not sorry for it," is not the implication one of relief that "the giants" have had their day, too? Do not Carlyle and Macaulay, as long as they are brilliant in the public eye, remind him painfully of his missing the mark? With them in the background, will not his own shortcoming in stature be less conspicuous? For his style in his *Fortnightly* period was not quiet; it was grand, with the best features of classical prose adapted to the modern temper. Furthermore, a comparison of it with Macaulay's or with Carlyle's (that of Carlyle's "Voltaire" or

his "Burns," not his *Sartor Resartus* or his *French Revolution*)
shows unmistakably—and this completes the whole truth about
his style in 1871—that he had felt the impact of both the giants.
He was no imitator, and *Voltaire* is the better for that; but the
breadth of vocabulary, the vigor in movement, the finality of
pronouncement, the keenness and distinctiveness of mind in
seeing traits and arguments in new lights, the particular kind
of picturesqueness in much of the figurative language, all show
how strong and durable the impression of Macaulay and Carlyle was when he read them at Oxford.

ROUSSEAU

All that has been said of the purpose and nature of *Voltaire*
holds true as well of *Rousseau*. Morley undertook the study
because there was "no full biographical account of the man in
English," and Frederic Harrison complimented him on its success because he knew no work which contained so much "at
once central and scientific about the problems" of their own
time. Rousseau, too, was illuminated against a background of
the 1870's.

In its literary merit *Rousseau* ranks close to *Voltaire*, distinguished by the same brilliant, high level of style. Morley's
talent for telling phrases was never more active; his phrase-
ology is incontestably charged and accurate, difficult to resist
quoting. In addition to sharply tempered prose, there is again
much nobly ecclesiastical in tone, as when Rousseau is identified as one of "those singular spirits who come from time to
time to quicken the germs of strange thought and shake the
quietness of the earth."

Most of the chief themes of *Voltaire* are echoed in *Rousseau*.
At the outset Morley pleads for broadmindedness and tolerance
in considering the great confessionist, who can be appraised
only by the mind which is "open and liberal" and whose "vo-

cabulary is enlarged beyond the pedantic formulas of unreal ethics." The frankness with which he discusses Rousseau's erotic aberrations is commendable. No prude, but averse to placarding physiological data, he stresses the lesson which licentiousness teaches humanity. Mme. de Warens, who was extra-maritally attached to Rousseau and who, after sinking into abandoned promiscuity, died in poverty and wretchedness, is almost lurid proof that "the old hoary world" values continence, along with prudence and honesty, because "the breach of such virtues is ever in the long run deadly to mutual trust, to strength, to freedom, to collectedness, which are the reserve of humanity against days of ordeal." Over the escapade involving Rousseau and Mme. de Houdetot, an affair which precipitated the *Nouvelle Héloise*, Morley cannot stifle his disgust and he justifiably sums it all up in one of the most picturesque verdicts he ever wrote: "a scene of moral humiliation that half sickens, half appals, and we turn away with dismay as from a vision of the horrid loves of heavy-eyed and scaly shapes that haunted the warm, primeval ooze." There is the expected censure of non-humanitarian church dogma, too. Rousseau's begetting of illegitimate children can be condoned, for, in bequeathing them to institutions, he acted charitably, but the Christian clergy, on the other hand, can never be forgiven for commanding ignorant church members through the centuries to burden the world with thousands of children, incontinently produced and destined to squalor. A good deal of Comtism as well pervades the work; humanity is depicted struggling toward a millennium, which, it is acknowledged, will require "uncounted myriads of lives, and immeasurable geologic periods of time, for its high and beneficent consummation."

But certain new notes are sounded in *Rousseau*. Criticism, it is stated explicitly, ought to "separate what is accidental in form, transitory in manner, and merely local in suggestion, from the general ideas that live under a casual and particular literary robe." Too fine a concern with details of style or construction, too strong a preoccupation with idiosyncrasies of an author's character or conduct are bad and do nothing but encourage "poverty of spirit." "Larger impressions and more durable meanings" are alone important in appraisal, and a critic can understand an author only by "advancing to the central elements" of his being. So Rousseau's central elements are early summed up in a brilliantly written picture of "the type of character that lay unfolded in the youth of seventeen." Rousseau was fundamentally a paradox: "a vagrant sensuous temperament, strangely compounded with Genovese austerity; an ardent and fantastic imagination, incongruously shot with threads of firm reason; too little conscience and too much. . . ." To him recollection was much sweeter than actual experience, and images more titillating than facts, because "his rational part was fatally protected by a non-conducting envelope of sentiment" which "intercepted clear ideas on their passage, and even cut off the direct and true impress of those objects and their relations, which are the material of clear ideas."

Rousseau conveys Morley's denunciation of censorship in literature. Certain books are undoubtedly inflammatory for children; the Bible in this respect is as dangerous as the *Nouvelle Héloise*. But this does not mean that they ought to be kept from adults or never written. The most consequential human relationship and the most far-reaching human passion are as vital to literature as to life, and so-called incendiary books must be acknowledged to treat them frankly. A censorship to extirpate them would be a "puerile doctrine that must emasculate literature and art." Besides, immorality is a relative thing and must be looked at historically. Although the *Nouvelle Héloise* shocked a public nourished on the milk diet of pure Victorian literature, "to the people who read Crébillon and *La Pucelle,* it was without doubt elevating." This is not to say, of course, that all the loathsome, garbaged details about perverted human instincts and emotions ought to be paraded on the printed page. Morley, it is true, could assert, "In any case, let us know the facts about human nature, and the pathological facts no less than the others. These are the first thing, and the second, and the third also." But here he meant that such facts are indispensable to the physician and the psychiatrist for their understanding and successful treatment of mentally sick men and women; in the craft of writing they have no part to play.

The *Nouvelle Héloise* is laudable as a picture of idealized domesticity, an arraignment of all that was bad in the domestic service of the old aristocratic order; it marks "a beginning of true democracy, as distinguished from the mere pulverisation of aristocracy" and implies "the essential priority of social over political reform." This opinion is in keeping with Morley's insistence that Rousseau was more potent as a social than a political force, and *Emile* ("one of the seminal books in the history of literature") more influential than *The Social Contract.*

Rousseau's scheme of education contains serious faults. It places far too much emphasis on self-love as a motivating force with no provision at all for curbing it. It would result in individuals reared on egotism who, with no respect for society and utter contempt for authority, would soon transform any social state into a "moral wilderness." Products of an instruction depending almost exclusively on stratagem and "artificially contrived circumstances," they would further lack what it was imperative they should develop—"spontaneousness of habit," the result only of complete sympathy between pupil and teacher. Not that Morley, never overcredulous about human nature, believed it possible to appeal to the embryonic reason of children. The "firm and promptly acting habit," which must be acquired early, would derive from their being taught by good example to act through the "desire to please."

Despite his understanding, however, of a character anti-
thetically different from his own, Morley's attitude is hardly
one of admiration. In the long run, Rousseau's lack of the
historical sense, his emotional abandon, which in his *Confessions* was "more revolting in its self-feeling" than anything
ever written by monk or saint, and his "pernicious" views on
women, whom he craved to place in a "semi-philosophic seraglio," rendered him deplorable. Once in a letter, Morley
wrote, though not in the highest seriousness, that "pity is the
right mind in which to think of the miserable wretch."

One wonders, in conclusion, whether Morley's extreme consciousness of himself as one of the rationalistic élite and his
aversion to vulgarity and cheapness did not leave a more pre-
dominantly intellectual stamp on *Rousseau* than is good for it.
Considering himself a writer for a chosen few, he doubted in
1873 whether there was "much of a public for this kind of
work in England, or anywhere else out of Paris." As a result,
is there not something in the prose of *Rousseau* perilously close
to the very "overleaping ambition" he later counseled against,
as disastrous in literature "as in so many other things"? The
striking phrases are almost too many, the brilliance is almost
too consistent in its cerebral sharpness and dexterity. With
little relaxation possible, the reader has the constant impression
of confronting a mind tense and unflagging in its process of
analysis.

DIDEROT

Morley's two-volume work on Diderot and the Encyclopedists in 1878 closed his series of French studies. More descriptive than either *Voltaire* or *Rousseau*, its special function was
to bring the "social significance and positive quality of the
group into the prominence" they deserved. About the general
character of the eighteenth century, however, and its great
problems and attainments in philosophy, science, politics, and

religion, it says nothing more final or illuminating than has already been said in *Voltaire* or *Rousseau*. For example, after a comprehensive exposition of Holbach's *System of Nature*, Morley is forced not only to admit that Holbach lacked a "positive" view of history but also to call "the disregard of historic opinion the natural defect of material speculation from Epicurus downwards." With the important generalizations concerning it already decisively laid down, *Diderot* helps the reader to see the age more clearly as a whole by reiterating and filling in with much detail. In literary quality it is not climactic for it lacks the brilliance and animation of *Voltaire* and *Rosseau*. There are passages in it which leave the impression that Morley has not yet caught his breath after the pace of his two preceding studies; frequently he avoids detailed explanations of topics by referring to definitive statements to be found in one or the other of them.

Much of *Diderot* is inescapably occupied with religion, about which Morley commits himself in his accustomed way. The gentleness of the rationalistic attack on the Church of England in the 1870's, almost startling after the use by Frenchmen against the Catholic Church of "those more brutal weapons in controversy" a century before, he attributes to Wordsworth's poetry and the Oxford tracts, which had tempered the Anglican Church and given it "an equity, a breadth, an elevation, a pensive grace" it had never had before. The habitual bold indictment of Catholicism and defense of the Revolution are accompanied in *Diderot* by the assertion that all the crimes and blood of the French cataclysm are only a drop in comparison with the fanatical excesses with which the church has stained the book of history. And Morley, deploring like Mill before him the fact that the breakdown of belief in God is so often accompanied by a collapse ethically, explains that it is impossible to build sound ethics "on the shifting sands and rotting foundations of theology."

In an assay of the influence of science on men's lives, Diderot
is classified as a "social destroyer by accident, but in intention
. . . a truly scientific moralist, penetrated by the spirit of observation and experiment." Praise of his candor and baldness in
dissection, however, leads into a consideration of his psychology, and then, inevitably, into the basic field of sex and sexual
ethics. Censorship, it is repeated, is wholly bad, but a line must
be drawn somewhere, and good taste is the only agency to help
a man draw it. The scientific laboratory is one thing; the literary page another. Diderot's attempt "to give an air of polite
comedy to functions and secretions must be pronounced detesta-
ble." He is also to be censured for advocating the abolition of
marriage. If society is to hold together, the units composing it
must be stable; abolish the home, and society topples. For the
home rests on a foundation, too—the moral integrity of the
man and woman who organize it; and they can have no integrity if they reduce their attraction "to its purely physical elements" and return to the "nakedness of the brute"; the moral
associations clustered around the relationship must be maintained.

Diderot's penetrating understanding of women stands in
fortunate contrast to Rousseau's superficial and immoral conception of them, and his admirable habit of suspending judgment, a "reasoned leniency," can be associated with the breadth
of mind of Burke. His great pity, too, is commendable, for
Morley's favorite aphorism, engraved over the fireplace in the
library of his home and used time and time again in his writing,
was one by Bacon: "The nobler a soul is, the more objects of
compassion it hath." Diderot's prose, however, is prevented by
too much German heaviness and dispersiveness from ranking
with the best French of his period. He had realized, creditably,
the need for greater realism in drama and had carried out his
ideas with a certain success in his *Père de Famille*; but the
dialogue he had contrived in imitation of everyday, "natural"

speech was intolerably vapid, and his didacticism had kept him from perceiving "that virtue may be made attractive without pulling the reader or the spectator by the sleeve and urgently shouting in his ear how attractive virtue is." Moreover, monumental as was his achievement with the *Encyclopedia*, he had not always written what he believed and had been occasionally guilty of faulty classification, bad proportioning, and frequent digression. Finally, as a social teacher, he exhibits two great deficiencies: he had failed to see "the guiding idea of the unity of the intellectual history of man, and the organic integrity of thought," and, like Victor Hugo after him, he had mistakenly "poured fulminant denunciations" on Society in the abstract instead of impressing, as did the greatest English thinkers from Milton to Mill, "new ideas on the Individual" and exacting a "vigorous personal answer to the moral and spiritual call."

The French studies show convincingly that Morley's critical method places his subjects in sharp relief against a broad historical background. So Rousseau, considered in relation to social speculation before and after his time as well as in terms of the social theory of his own day, is found wanting, because he was blind to all the antecedents of the very contemporary thought and custom which he wanted to uproot at a pulling, but which, to be understood, needed to be traced back through centuries. Conveniently shortsighted, he could see only the imagined perfect state of nature before civilization began and the idealized state that would spring magically into existence after the present social system was remade. There was no continuity in his conception, and no soundness in his speculation; all the complexities involved in growth were beyond him. But to Morley, whose thinking was colored by Darwinian theory, growth was all-important; no institution, like no organism, could be considered apart from its evolution.

Criticism, then, had widened its scope. It was no longer what

it had often been in the hands of Samuel Johnson—a judgment
according to "taste," the impressing of a powerful enlightened
personality in domination over the minds about him. And it
had grown beyond the appraising of Macaulay, brilliant and
fascinating as that had been, because Macaulay had too often
focused on biographical highlights and been too often prone to
narrow moral classification. Not that Morley, although intent
in his criticism on substituting *"becoming* for *being,* the relative
for the absolute, dynamic movement for dogmatic immobility,"
was without fixed principles of evaluation. Scientifically as he
subordinated the character of a writer to a patient search for
his ideas and an analysis of their relationship to the intellectual
currents of his own age, the criteria by which he judged the
worth of the writer to humanity were the beliefs he himself held
as an advanced Liberal. And as his temper and method are well
illustrated by the French studies, so is his vehicle, his prose
style, distinguished by "constant precision of phrase—elaborate sustention of argument."

THE POLITICAL BIOGRAPHIES

Since to Morley, no less than to Arnold, literature was a
criticism of life, one of "the great humanizing arts," his political biographies of Burke, Cobden, Walpole, Cromwell, and
Gladstone, are not irrelevant to a consideration of his critical
activity. Apart from their value as lives of distinguished English statesmen, they are worth while for what they reveal of his
"multiplicity of sympathies" and "steadiness of sight." They
confirm, one discovers, all that the French studies disclosed.
His wide sympathy among personalities is evident, of course,
merely from a glance at some of the different historical figures
who engaged him: Rousseau, Voltaire, De Maistre, Robespierre, Cromwell, Cobden, Walpole, Gladstone. Recognizing

his own adaptability very early, he had described it to Harrison almost vivaciously: "I am by nature vagrant and bee-like, gathering honey (and acids) from every subject that opens." His "steadiness of sight" in the biographies is equally evident; they maintain all the values in life which he early learned to cherish and the objectives of criticism illustrated in the French studies.

In general, the writing in this English series lacks the sustained force of the earlier group. The two treatments of Burke are exceptions, and *Cromwell*, too, in certain respects, is not markedly inferior, but *Cobden*, *Walpole*, and *Gladstone* are reticently and soberly, frequently dully, written, with nothing of the luster of *Rousseau* or *Voltaire*. The fact that, as outgrowths of his preoccupation with politics, they became laden with dates and facts, is partly responsible for the decline. Furthermore, Cobden and Gladstone as contemporaries left an abundance of biographical materials, much of which, in writing their lives, he considered it appropriate to utilize, withdrawing himself almost completely. Equally consequential is his feeling about biography, to which *Cobden* and *Gladstone*, since they are more biographical than the shorter studies of Walpole, Burke, and Cromwell, would be expected more strictly to conform. He always insisted that it was not the biographer's task to "rake among the private obscurities of even first-rate men," but to keep himself as much as he could "in contact with what is great." In other words, biography, like the best in other kinds of literature, should edify; and what edifies is not the full-drawn physical picture of a man, but an exposition of the principles by which he acted. Moreover, it is questionable whether Morley ever felt himself equipped to write biography, because for years he conscientiously refrained from undertaking what would profess to be one. In the "hands of a man of the requisite capacity and sensibility," biography was probably supreme among all forms of prose, but one could "almost count upon one's fingers the really good" specimens of it in English literature. Not many lives, either, would inspire such masterpieces. And so he had announced in the preface to *Edmund Burke* that he would devote himself not to a reproduction of the man but to a historical "criticism of his . . . relations, and contributions to the main transactions of his time." Finally, there is this to say, that the older Morley grew, the more firmly did he believe no biography able to penetrate a man and reveal his inmost self, in the face of his complexities and hidden streams of character. "The half of us," he maintained, "is misunderstanding, even between those who are most close to one another, and whom the action most concerns."

BURKE

Morley's attachment to Edmund Burke was lifelong. He was stirred in making his earliest study of the great statesman, spoke of him twenty years later as "the most majestic of them all," and only five years before his death was still reading him with exclamation: "He is a great theme. What a mind! His fame grows greater with time! Macaulay was right when he said of certain passages, 'How divine!' " The first study, *Edmund Burke*, appearing in instalments in *The Fortnightly Review* in 1867, was published later that year and by 1876 had been reviewed in one source "as equal to Macaulay's little biographies." A second presentation, *Burke* (1879), although it lacks the earlier volume's excellent section on the French Revolution and possesses considerably more information about Burke's personal and literary life, is, in its ideas, substantially the same.

Despite the fact that Burke had had much of the rationalist in him, he had hated the "very sound of metaphysical distinctions" and abstract systems. He had insisted that political panaceas were futile, that government measures must be tried through practice and made to suit man's nature "as modified by his habits." He had seen the indispensability, along with acute intellectual habits, of moral and spiritual ideals in life; he had distrusted logic as a single, guiding force and written that unsparing, malevolent use of it could blast every human ideal and institution. He had been liberal in much of his attitude toward the people—liberal without being democratic: he had championed the cause of the Americans in the Revolutionary crisis by saying that an English victory would prove fatal in the end to the liberties of England itself, and he had declared: "Whenever the people have a feeling, they commonly are in the right; they sometimes mistake the physician." He had had some conception of the continuity of history, and in writing of the traditions and functions of social classes in England, had shown "moral, historic, conservative imagination, in which order, social continuity, and the endless projection of past into present, and of present into future are clothed with the sanctity of an inner shrine." He had believed in the goodness of the majority of mankind, too; there had been no retrogression in his scheme of things. He had seen the importance of order: liberty with order in the state being equivalent to justice, and order in the individual's own life to be secured through what he called "just prejudice," prejudice with latent reason in it, rendering "a man's virtue his habit, and not a series of unconnected acts." To him also the establishment of dignity and integrity was the basic essential for a life that was to be more than "a meaningless parcel of thrums."

Even though Burke had prized peace above truth, Morley found him in these other important respects a great-minded, great-souled man. Furthermore, he had been an exemplary combination of the man of action and the man of letters, showing, "like some other men" in English history, "that books are a better preparation for statesmanship than early training in the subordinate posts and among the permanent officials of a public department." His fervid, magnificent style was admirable "because his sentiment was lofty," but those passages of it were to be preferred where reason, judgment, and lucidity, not declamation, produced the "effects of eloquence."

Edmund Burke, then, early though it came, was one of Morley's most significant books. First, it was a clear, vigorous, and full presentation of the character of the great statesman, neither idolatrous nor prolix, which, in demonstrating the consistency of his ideas throughout his career, disproved the general notion that he had moved from liberality in his youth to reactionaryism in his old age. It showed that fundamentally he had been conservative in his earliest days, and that, despite his intense hatred of the French Revolution in his decline, he was not shifting further to the right in damning it. Second, the book was a revelation of the base of conservatism in Morley himself and should have shown outraged defamers of *Voltaire* and *Rousseau* in 1871 and 1873 that for England, no less than for Heaven, he advocated order as a first law.

COBDEN

The Life of Richard Cobden, published in 1881, was a commemoration of one of the greatest of the century's Liberal leaders, yet, despite its preoccupation with politics, it is not too confined in interest. There was much in Cobden that Morley found to admire, much that he discovered they had in common. Despite his common birth, Cobden, too, had been graceful, idealistic, dignified, and well-read. He had known and liked French and had become the friend of Prosper Mérimée. Morally opposed to slavery, he had denounced the secession of the South in America in 1861. His political experience had led him to condemn English imperialism, to hate force as a governmental policy, to admire "Prussian efficiency and intelligence," to criticize the British Constitution as too much "a thing of monopolies and churchcraft and sinecures, armorial hocus-pocus, primogeniture and pageantry," and to plead for toler-ance and a degree of self-government for the Irish, contending pertinently that if Catholic and Protestant could not "live together in Belfast, excepting under something like martial law," the English were not the people "to teach Christian char-ity and tolerance to the Hindoos." Morley's own experience had led him by 1881 to all of these stands. Still able in 1912 to declare that the essential in any community was "a grand re-serve of wise, thoughtful, unselfish, longsighted men and wo-men" with "parliamentary power enough," he had every reason, thirty-one years earlier, to feel himself one with Cobden, who had insisted that it was not the franchise but an enlightened electorate, not a revolution but the schoolhouse, that could effect a change for the better in England and make it permanent. Cobden had sympathized with women, too, and believed that as the doctrine of physical force lost favor and a belief in moral power succeeded it, they would "gain in the scale." Not pro-fessionally religious, he had nevertheless confessed that, by nature, he had much "veneration" and a "sympathy for men who act under that impulse," because he reverenced it "as the great leverage which had moved mankind to powerful action"; no man, theologian or scientist, could do more than profess "to act on the morality of the New Testament." And these sentences which he wrote about the dedication of his life might almost have been written by Morley himself: "At all events, let us remember that to live usefully is far better than living long. And do not let us deprive ourselves of the gratification at last, a gratification which the selfish never have, that we have not embittered our whole lives with heaping up money, but that we have given a part of our time to more rational and worthy exertions."

The worth of *The Life of Richard Cobden* is better realized when *Walpole* is compared with it. Since *Walpole*, too, is a political biography, one would like to believe that it would never have been written had Morley not been acting as self-appointed literary commemorator for his party. Unfortunately, this wish is not borne out by fact. Because Walpole, long before Britain's expulsion of the French from the New World, had rejected a parliamentary proposal to tax colonists in America, Morley, in his twenties, considered him a "profoundly sagacious" man. Yet what value could have resided for him in the eighteenth-century minister, beyond certain political tendencies which he exemplified, it is impossible to see. Published in 1884, three years after *Cobden*, his book marks a retrogression in literary worth and human interest. It was apparently not remembered as a labor of love, for Morley rarely spoke of it later, never quoted from it or alluded to themes in it as he was accustomed to do with certain of his others. Walpole as a man was his antithesis, and nothing in his life was matter for great literature, literature of edification. He had no "moral dignity in his character" and his social conduct would have made him intolerable to Victorians; he was without an "elevated imagination" and in his speeches was never "truly eloquent"; and even though he gave a pension to the poet Young, offered one to Pope, and subscribed for copies of Fielding's work, he "looked upon writing as a mechanical business," took no delight in reading, and called musicians "a pack of fiddlers." Spiritually and aesthetically he was benighted. To see anything at all of merit in him, Morley recommends that men of action be judged "by the standards of men of action." Walpole had possessed the three necessary qualifications of a "chief minister"—acute judgment, wide knowledge of the "business in hand," and tenacious will; and fifty-five years before Adam Smith he had advised that trade be made "as practicable and as easy as may be." Through his "penetration and rapidity" he had defeated a bill that would have given the House of Lords "a fixed preponderance of power over Crown and Commons alike," and he had made "a long stride towards establishing the doctrine of Cabinet solidarity." For so setting his "deep stamp" on the form of English government he deserved lasting commendation.

CROMWELL

The character of Oliver Cromwell, at once authoritarian and liberal, had long attracted Morley. In July, 1900 he published a strong-lined presentation of it in a volume which, good as it is, he asserted he would never have brought out had he known in time of the historian Gardiner's more comprehensive undertaking. In its impression *Cromwell* reminds one strongly of *Burke*, not only because of occasional comparisons of the two men or of their statements (Cromwell's "In the government of nations, that which is to be looked after is the affections of the people" might have come "straight out of Burke"), but because of Morley's reaction to Cromwell's character, too, which, as in the case of Burke, is one of deep esteem before his breadth of sight, his practical-mindedness, and his expansive soul. Not trying to overlook or excuse but only regretting, he equitably introduces the reactionaryism of his subject and gives it unbiased consideration. His frankness in handling the narrowing change which overtook the great leader and the brutal excesses which stained his dictatorship is creditable. Yet despite Cromwell's unfortunate deeds, many of his early declarations, unprecedented among statesmen in their humanity, ring unforgettably for Morley—and for the reader, too, after he has closed the volume. It was the Protector who had decreed, "It will be found an unjust and unwise jealousy to deprive a man of his natural liberty upon a supposition he may abuse it." Mor-

ley's own last word on him, "what in a single sentence defines
the true place of Cromwell in our history," is that, in a time of
crisis, he struck for unity of the state and liberty and "crushed
the absolutist pretensions alike of crown and mitre."

GLADSTONE

To *The Life of William Gladstone* (1903) is attached a
problem similar to that of *Walpole*. Granted that the task of
composing the biography was a commission from the crown,
why did Morley consider it a labor of love and a venerative
tribute? Huxley had summed up Gladstone as the man who
had debased "the greatest intellect in Europe" by "simply following majorities and the crowd," and since Morley was of
Huxley's school, should he not have felt the same way about
the prime minister? Indeed, in the early *Fortnightly* days,
though he had praised Gladstone on at least one occasion for
his industry, official knowledge, financial ingenuity, and love
of improvement, he had not hesitated at other times to stigma-
tize his mind as a "busy mint" for coining "logical counter-
feits" and to denounce him because, in his fondness for "be-
wildering words or impotent silence," he "never took up a
decided line about foreign affairs but once in his life, and that
was when he declared with a terseness as unprecedented with
him as it was unlucky, that the Southern slaveholders were
made into a nation." In the light of his *Fortnightly* contempt
for that "fund of brutal, stubborn biblicalism in our Briton"
and "that den of hypocrites and thieves at Westminster" did
Morley later perjure himself in office under one of the most
pious, most orthodox high-church statesmen England had ever
had? To all of this the answer is, no. The affection which he
developed for Gladstone was genuine, and the praise in a passage like the following, written after a conversation with him,
is sincere.

I return to my room with the sensations of a man who has taken delightful exercise in fresh air. He is so wholly free from the ergoteur [quibbler]. . . . He fits his tone to the thing; he can be as playful as anybody. . . . He cannot resist rising in an instant to the general point of view—to grasp the elemental considerations of character, history, belief, conduct, affairs. . . . I never knew anybody less guilty of the tiresome sin of arguing for victory.

With Huxley's previously quoted remark, Morley, certainly by the late 1870's when he came to know Gladstone intimately, had no sympathy. Between his early *Fortnightly* days and his tenure as Irish Secretary under the prime minister, he had grown to realize, it must be remembered, the limitations and the dangers of the exclusively scientific outlook; physical scientists had proved as narrow in their point of view as theologians were in theirs. Social devotion and political principle were more indicative than scientific ardor of worth of character; "harmony of aim, not identity of conclusion," he averred in *On Compromise*, "is the secret of the sympathetic life." Gladstone's earnestness, then, and his objectives as a great party leader drew Morley to him. The two had also in common a deep love of books—of the classics in particular; and Gladstone was, in a limited sense, an author in his own right. Still influential, too, was Morley's basic devoutness, never uprooted, by which, Harrison informed him as early as 1876, Gladstone was "seriously, deeply impressed," and by which he himself was prompted to recognize in the statesman evidences of wholesomeness and breadth and to acknowledge that he "quite felt his attraction."

The biography is expressly concerned with Gladstone's growth into a Liberal and avoids any exploration of his theological history. "What is extraordinary . . . is . . . that with a steadfast tread he marched along the high anglican road to the summits of that liberalism which it was the original object of the anglicans to resist and overthrow." Painstakingly it traces Gladstone's development from the Tory who in 1833 voted for the worst clauses of an Irish Coercion Bill, was against the admission of Jews to Parliament, opposed the admission of dissenters to universities, voted emphatically for the Corn Laws, protected military and naval sinecures, defended shorter parliaments, and condemned the ballot; through the maturing thinker who in 1842 was pledging his life to "the external warfare against ignorance and depravity"; to the retired prime minister, a confirmed Liberal, who could look back with satisfaction on the incitement he had given to the Italian movement for independence and the progress he had made in the direction of Home Rule for Ireland. Gladstone had had to discover Liberty for himself; it had never been taught to him at Oxford.

Gladstone's three thick volumes continue the method used in *The Life of Richard Cobden*. There is hardly anything of the biographer in the printed matter; Gladstone speaks for himself through his diaries and letters, of which there were originally thousands of pages to be perused before *The Life* was begun. That Morley's burden was tremendous is, unfortunately, still felt in his production. It is cumbersome, laborious, factually too heavy, politically too involved, dead under its own weight. It is no "masterpiece in biography" at all, as some critics would have it, but a patient, correct achievement in documentary organization.

THE CRITICAL ESSAYS

Struck by his review of *Les Travaillers de la Mer* in 1866, Victor Hugo complimented Morley in a letter for clearly understanding his ideas and faultlessly interpreting the whole book for the English public. The literary relationship that ensued, enduring until Hugo's death, was featured by Morley's impressive review of *Quatre-Vingt Treize* in 1874 and his meeting with the great poet-novelist in 1879. This early review, along with articles on Meredith and George Eliot, marked the beginning of a long series of essays in criticism similar to those of Carlyle, Macaulay, and Matthew Arnold. The strongest and most memorable of these appeared in *The Fortnightly* during his editorship, yet he wrote some very good pieces in the 1880's after entering politics. Several of the lot are reprinted in prose anthologies today—that on Macaulay most frequently—and eleven of them he thought well enough of to include in the volume, *Critical Miscellanies*, when his works were being published by Macmillan and Company in 1921. Those that concern major figures in English literature still possess considerable interest and value as expressions of the critical attitude consistent through the French studies and the English biographical series.

CARLYLE

"Industrious study of other authors," Morley had proclaimed in 1865, "is the surest preventive against that washiness, and thinness and languor" which are bad writing. Among those whom he had studied was Carlyle, for it was while he was still at Oxford that Carlyle, in helping awaken him to the problems of society, had shown him what vehement, prophetic prose could do in making an argument forceful. Never for a moment forgetting, however, that "it is not everybody who can bend the bow of Ulysses," in the pages of *The Fortnightly* he had warned rash aspirants to the feat:

. . . Mr. Carlyle's style, potent as it is in his own books, becomes in the hands of other people as the manna which was preserved in the wilderness until the next day after it descended from heaven. In style as in other things, the corruption of the best is the worst.

Still, in spite of his rigorous aversion to imitation, Morley had been influenced; the confident, pontifical tone of his declarations of the 1870's indicates that he considered himself the raiser of the fallen mantle and was determined to write his way to the side of the highest. He never ceased to be conscious of Carlyle's "penetrating, imaginative genius."

The philosophical limitations of Carlyle described in his essay in 1871 are what turned Morley away for good after his visit a year later "to the old man, with whom" he "had never had a word before." "Silent and discipular," he wincingly endured three-quarters of an hour of praise of Goethe, Schiller, and Jean Paul, and heard *The Fortnightly* denounced as a "nest of cackatreeces," and then with no "instruction, or hint, or inspiration—not a jot or tittle," returned to London, convinced that there was "nothing precise or definite" about the aging scolder. So, in the essay, Carlyle is summed up as a "born poet," imaginatively effulgent, benevolently inclined, but incapable of coping effectively with the complex problems of English society. With him "thought is an aspiration, and justice a sentiment, and society a retrogression," in which characteristic he is a sensibilist working on the same principles as Rousseau. His trust in moral earnestness, in working and being silent, is worthless. What he complains against in "Shooting Niagara: and After" as "torpid unveracity of heart" is not the fault at bottom; unveracity itself, "torpid or fervid," breeds "intellectual dimness, and it is this last which prevents us from seeing a way out of the present ignoble situation. We need light more than heat." Furthermore, he deals too frequently in abstractions to be clear or reliable, and in his attitude with regard to heroes, dangerously close to a belief in might as right, is more reactionary than De Maistre himself. As a philosopher, all that he can be valued for are his relatively broad moral attitude in judging men, his fight against the dogmatic temper in religion, "because this is work that goes deeper than to assail dogmas," and his help in strengthening and raising "the conscious and harmonious dignity of humanity."

Significant in the essay are frequent phrases which, striking and picturesque, might not inconceivably have been struck off by Carlyle himself. Thus, Carlyle's definition of the Great Man (the "light which enlightens," etc.) is identified as "only another form of the anthropomorphic conceptions of deity" and the pronouncement comes that "in that house there are many mansions, the boisterous sanctuary of a vagabond polytheism." Carlylism itself is "the male of Byronism. It is Byronism with thew and sinew, bass pipe and shaggy bosom." And Carlyle, despite the fact that he was followed by other teachers more intelligible and more reliable, is almost apotheosized in the line: "Here was the friendly fire-bearer who first conveyed the Promethean spark, here the prophet who first smote the rock."

This early essay is not Morley's last word on Carlyle. In November, 1885, upon the appearance of Froude's biography of the great Scot, he wrote an article-review in *Macmillan's*, "The Man of Letters as Hero." Here he states that, though ordinarily a writer's private life, like that of any other artist or statesman, ought to be exempt from public scrutiny, the case is different of a man who, posing as a prophet with an invaluable message of his own, has tried to tell other people how to live. Carlyle deserves to have his miserable personal existence exposed, and his pitiable incapacity to make anything harmonious of his own life laid bare. His ruthless slurring of his contemporaries, his inability to penetrate beneath exteriors were to Morley unforgivable, and his "tone in speaking of a man who was so much superior to him in so many ways as Mill, is simply painful." His self-styled "serious turn of mind" was in reality only "an everlasting torrent of inhuman scolding." His rage and his indiscriminate anathematizing of everything in the world, after he had earlier damned the French rationalists of the eighteenth century for a pack of atheists, revealed that "in many respects no atheism has ever been preached . . . of blacker dye" than his own. Morley quotes, and agrees with, Mazzini; Carlyle loved "calm and silence platonically"; his teaching and character would never incite anybody to love virtue. "The life of Emerson at Concord, and of Mill at Blackheath and Avignon, tends more to edification than the life of Carlyle, with all its tumultuous emotions, and all its strange celestial imaginings."

MACAULAY

In 1876, when he wrote his essay on Macaulay, nothing flattered Morley more than the request of *The Encyclopedia Britannica* for his "little piece" on Comte, which had followed close on the heels of his successful sketch of Burke. Tickled with the "hyperbole" of the Academy that *Burke* was the equal of Macaulay's little biographies, he wrote to Harrison to say that no praise could have meant more, "considering that Macaulay's little biographies in the Encyclopedia are about the most finished things he did." There is no denying his envy, at this time, of Macaulay's position in the field of critical biographical writing, no denying his intention of arriving at the same level, and on the strength of superior achievement. There is near-resentment in the brusque way he customarily dismissed Macaulay's vogue as due to a cheap flashiness and a titillating of the public's palate.

Macaulay can never be forgotten, Morley avows in his essay, for the stamp he set on style, style "in its widest sense, not merely on the grammar and mechanism of writing"; it is for that and for his genius in narration that English literature owes him a debt. Philosophically, though, he is worthless—contemptible to one of Mill's school. He had an "unanalytical turn of mind," was one of "the middle-class crowd in his heart," was complacent about the state of England, and would have voted with Anytus and Meletus against Socrates. He was arrogant and militant in his approach of Truth, used to knocking her down and dragging her after him by the hair of the head, "a prisoner of war and not a goddess." Alongside the high genius of Carlyle, he is meretricious; though he gives an "appearance of dignity and elevation," he has nothing underneath it but a "resolute and ostentatious common sense of a slightly coarse sort." Spiritually, he is lacking; he never rises to the elevated music made in literature "by the repressed trouble of grave and high souls."

This is the substance of Morley's judgment. What gives it a peculiar interest is that it reflects exactly what he ascribed to Macaulay, an "aptitude for forcing things into firm outline." Macaulay's goal, strong effects, is his own here, and he strikes out again and again with vehement figures which, as in his essay on Carlyle, are not at all alien to the giant predecessor he is discussing. This one, for example, censures Macaulay's flashy shallowness: "The wine of truth is in his cup a brandied draught, a hundred degrees above proof, and he too often replenishes the lamp of knowledge with naphtha instead of fine oil."

BYRON

Morley's memorably different treatment of Byron in 1877 illustrates excellently what he had said "synthetic criticism" ought to do: to see the poet against the background of his age, to relate him concretely to the movements of its social and political thought, and then trace the relations of his ideas, "either direct or indirect . . . to the visible tendencies of an existing age." For him Byron is pre-eminently the poet of the Revolution, the chief interpreter "of the moral tumult of the epoch," and he quotes Mazzini to show what an impetus he exerted in Italy. In so far as poetry is "the power of transfiguring action, character, and thought in the serene radiance of the purest imaginative intelligence; and the gift of expressing those transformed products in the finest articulate vibrations of emotional speech," he is constrained to acknowledge Shelley as Byron's superior, but he contends that the proof of Byron's genius is that his force was able to make so much of "elements so intrinsically unfavourable to high poetry as doubt, denial, antagonism, and weariness." To the greatest English poets, Shakespeare and Milton, for example, who were inspired by political and social themes above the spiritual motivation at bottom, Byron is allied in that he, too, was strongly concerned with "ideas of government and the other external movements of men in society, and with the play of the sentiments which spring from them." Despite his eccentricities and extravagance in behavior, it was because he had this broad social awareness and was sincere and fundamentally sober and rational enough to be kept "substantially straight, real, and human," that his appeal was so universal.

Byron is exemplary for his "sound view of the importance of form" and his avoidance of "clownish savagery" or "barbarism," into which too many unfettered English poets since Shakespeare's day have fallen; his good taste is "collateral proof of the sanity and balance which marked the foundations of his character." And last, he must be considered to have approached the positive spirit in his predilection for dramatic composition. Drama, by its very nature, must be objective, with its creator standing "apart and unseen." It deals with no final causes but depends rather upon the interplay of character and situation, upon cause and effect, in short; and in it the law of self-evolvement ought to operate just as in "the greater drama of physical phenomena" which unfolds itself to the scientific observer. Byron's "rudimentary and unsuspected affinity with the more constructive and scientific side of the modern spirit," then, as well as his revolutionary thirst for action, may explain why he was irresistibly attracted to the drama.

EMERSON

Never so interested in American literature as he was in American society and politics, Morley was nevertheless con-

cerned about it from the days when he woke to the importance
of style until he could no longer read a page. Intellectually
aristocratic, he was relentless in the fight he waged against the
barbarities of American slang and "the hideous importations
from American newspapers." In Washington in 1867 he had
met Walt Whitman and gone on several night walks with him,
but Whitman's confidence in his destiny (a "felonious purpose"
of "packing off the courtly muses . . . bag and baggage") had
not convinced him that Lowell and Emerson and the other New
Englanders no longer held any message for the modern world.
On the contrary, he was inclined to feel that the last words of
promise might have been spoken by them.

When Emerson had crossed his path in his undergraduate
days at Oxford, Morley had been too young for him. His essay
of 1884, however, is a mature estimate of the poet, which,
through its acumen, presents him in a fresh light. Since Emerson was agitated by "an intellectual demand for intense and
sublimated expression" rather than by a passion for dithy-
rambs, and since he was an individualist, there were grounds
for his attracting Morley. But his "pure spiritualism" betrays
limitations in his intellectuality. His unconcern with reason,
his disregard of the conscious, acting will, his conviction that
"impulsive and spontaneous innocence is higher than the
strength to conquer temptation" are points of separation between him and Morley. One's spiritual constitution is never
independent of his physical organization, and, just as surely,
never independent "of the social conditions that close about
him from the instant of his birth." Emerson is laudable for
reacting against what was artificial and spurious in the eighteenth century, but, lamentably, he was blind to the great
achievements of its true rationalism. Still, despite his frequent
cloudiness, he is superior to Carlyle in the way out which he
proposes, for, instead of preaching "self will, mastery, force,
and violent strength," he lays all his trust in the "honest, manly,

simple, and emancipated character of the citizen." Furthermore, his feeling for science deserves special attention. He was alive to the reality of the survival of the fittest in Nature—his very phrases strike at it—and he was delighted to feel that "the natural universe of force and energy" is a "One and a Whole." With Tyndall Morley believes him to have been undaunted by the discoveries of science but to have assimilated and "transmuted them into the finer forms and warmer lines of an ideal world." As an artist working with words, however, he was guilty of frequent awkwardness or "uncouthness" and produced poetry which is not "inevitable."

GEORGE ELIOT

George Eliot is a special case; a "great and profound observer of human life," she was one of those whom, like Mill, Morley met early, knew long, and venerated. It was her own prose in 1866 which had helped him to arrive at a definition of style as the result of "brooding over ideas, not words." As a poet she could not be called successful; Morley had tried to think otherwise yet conscientiously could not escape the conclusion that her verse was "magnificent but unreadable." Her artistry lay in fiction, inseparable from her profound, day-to-day humanity. Intellectually alert, receptive, and thorough, morally constant, she had been absorbed by all the agitating questions of the day, scientific as well as religious and social, and had been painstaking in forming definite opinions about them. Her intellectual habits had developed in her the desirable "spirit of order and proportion" and she had seen clearly that "pity and fairness" were two virtues indispensable to improving the lot of mankind. Amid the world's evil and pain her intellectual honesty had prevented her from becoming soured by her religious disillusionment, and she had done what Morley himself was steadfast in trying to do: avoided make-believe, seen things as they are, stripped of all pretense, and lived bravely through her suffering "without opium . . . and with conscious, clear-eyed endurance." Reverencing humanity and believing in progress, she had held simple renunciation of evil insufficient and believed positive efforts to promote the welfare of some portion of mortals obligatory. In her faith she was superior to Mill himself, because she had been consistent and maintained her position unshaken, whereas Mill's admissions in his posthumous essays on religion had betokened a sorry falling-off. She had developed a sympathetic attitude toward sects and come to believe that, no matter what their varying theological tenets, their active striving toward good justified their being.

Her methods as a novelist were admirable in one respect, faulty in another. She was exemplary for her awareness of "the full stream of evolution, heredity, survival, and fixed inexorable law"; her characters, not arbitrarily fashioned and led through a series of incidents, were rooted in antecedent events and shown acting through the operation of the law of cause and effect. On the other hand, according to her own admission, she had always fixed a theme, a moral scheme of things, first, and then evolved her story, fitting it to her pattern. This way of creating was certainly inferior to that of a genius like Shakespeare. *Adam Bede* was one of her greatest achievements; *Daniel Deronda*, however, was not composed "under her brightest star" and contained, regrettably, a certain quality of mysticism. *Middlemarch* was a triumph. Morley had exclaimed to Harrison in 1872 over the acuteness with which it revealed to a "smug" English public that "its Protestant well-to-do optimism" was "a lie and a delusion." "There is a kind of Pharisaism in other things than religion—and *Middlemarch* touches this with a drop of acid."

George Eliot, in conclusion, though she had believed in progress, had not been an energumen over it. Material benefits had not been the be-all and end-all for her; with her historic sense, she had realized that great moral values inherited from the past must be preserved. Even though her writing could have shown more "fancy, illusion, enchantment," through her insistence on spiritual nobility she was a great fictional force, and Morley, in closing his essay, agrees with Mill that she will always remain a "wise, benignant soul" for all "right-judging men and women."

WORDSWORTH

As Morley's estimate of him in 1888 showed, Wordsworth, too, possessed some significance for a Liberal; he, too, could be considered in terms of the French Revolution, if only in a negative and limited way. Not of its spirit as was Byron, he was its renunciation—a complete Tory, socially and politically. Nevertheless, the ninth, tenth, and eleventh books of *The Prelude* are memorable for their picture of the Revolution; they "breathe the very spirit of the great catastrophe," and artistically they exhibit much of the sternness and grandeur of Greek tragedy.

Although Wordsworth's attitude toward Nature was unscientifically narrow and optimistic, he possessed an extraordinarily keen eye for describing it, in which respect only Byron and Tennyson among nineteenth-century poets could rank with him. In prosodic craftsmanship he had superiors, even among the so-called minor poets, but in the sort of verse which was not meant to intoxicate but to awaken "elements of composure deep and pure, and of self-government in a far loftier sense than the merely prudential," he was paramount in his age. His "special gift, his lasting contribution" was his genius for idealizing the natural world, for sensing the quiet life underlying the commonest objects and spiritualizing it, considering the universe an animate presence exerting a continual effect on man and "breathing grandeur upon the very humblest face of human life."

In addition to such full-length essays devoted to a criticism of the whole work of certain authors, Morley wrote a number of excellent shorter reviews of individual volumes by contemporary artists in poetry or prose. These less extensive pieces deserve mention, and even reprinting.

SWINBURNE

The earliest of these minor evaluations is the excellent "Mr. Swinburne's New Poems," an anonymous indictment in *The Saturday Review* for August 4, 1866, of Swinburne's *Poems and Ballads*, which, almost alone, caused the withdrawal of the volume from sale. Inexorably hostile to all "current notions of decency and dignity and social duty," Swinburne deserved credit for his audacity in revealing "to the world a mind all aflame with the feverish carnality of the schoolboy over the dirtiest passages in Lemprière," for it was "not everybody who could ask us all to go hear him tuning his lyre in a sty." While poetry should never be attenuated to such stuff as might innocuously be put in the hands of eighteen-year-old girls and used in Sunday schools, there was, nevertheless, "an enormous difference between an attempt to revivify . . . the grand old pagan conception of Joy and an attempt to glorify all the bestial delights that the subtleness of Greek depravity was able to contrive." For the time being, most of Swinburne's readers, not understanding the prurient references to Sappho, Messalina, and Hermaphroditus, would fortunately escape the taint of the "nameless and abominable." A second and a third such volume, however, would enable English maidens to "acquire a truly delightful familiarity with these unspeakable foulnesses," the excretions of a "putrescent imagination."

Apart from Swinburne's "nameless and shameless abominations," the evocativeness and the music of his verse were to be praised. Yet he was not real Greek. In the first place, whereas

the Greek poets had observed "scrupulous moderation and so-
briety in colour," he was too often disgustingly extravagant,
feverishly oppressive in his garish, lurid, violent palette. Furthermore, the Greeks had never lost sight of thought in their
lines; by contrast he was meretricious and could be discovered
frequently making a "trick of words and letters" and conceits
do "duty for thoughts."

As with thought, so with deep emotion. Passion in Swinburne
was only counterfeit, and amounted to no more than "mad
intoxicated sensuality." He was deficient indeed in his whole
attitude toward life. He knew the terrifying immensity of the
universe and man's pitiable insignificance and ephemerality in
it, but he could not do with that realization what a great poet
should: either transmute it into reverent awe and stir his readers to "solemn rapture" or else forge it into truly diabolical
negation, jeering and mocking at human beings "like an un-
clean fiery imp from the pit." He could do no more at best than
rise to prolix complaints about the futility of life, and at worst,
sink sweating into "schoolboy lustfulness."

MORRIS

In 1868, soon after the appearance of *The Earthly Paradise*,
Morley wrote a review of it in *The Fortnightly* in which,
acutely, he praised William Morris for his central quality, "a
vigorous and healthy objectivity; a vision and a fancy ever
penetrated by the colour and light and movement of external
things, just as they stir and penetrate the painter." Removed
from the spiritual perplexities and strife of his day, Morris had
made it his concern to look with freshness and simplicity on
nature in all her moods and to reproduce what he saw truth-
fully and precisely. He was to be commended for the absence
of artificiality and strain in his descriptions, for his sparing
use of simile (hitherto "supposed to be the peculiar figure of

the story-teller from Homer downwards"), and for his narrative, so "full of change and variety of personage and incident." Indeed, Morley did not think it too bold to predict that when *The Earthly Paradise* was completed, it might have "a longer duration in the minds and hearts of men than perhaps any contemporary verse," for it possessed an abundance of "those broad and unsophisticated moods that enchant men for all time."

BROWNING

The Ring and the Book, Morley found in 1869 to be technically marred by "harsh and formless lines, bursts of metrical chaos . . . passages marked by a coarse violence of expression . . . nothing short of barbarous"; such capricious grotesqueness, he was afraid, would lead to interminable aping among versifying lesser lights. But if there were unforgivable perversities, there were also unsurpassable passages of "sustained gravity" and noble diction, and the work certainly produced "that wide unity of impression which it is the highest aim of dramatic art, and perhaps of all art, to produce." Considered as a whole, it was beautiful, for did not beauty grow out of "such an arrangement and disposition of the parts of the work as, first kindling a great variety of dispersed emotions and thoughts in the mind of the spectator, finally concentrates them in a single mood of joyous, sad, meditative, or interested delight"?

For its substance even more than for its form, *The Ring and the Book* was to be welcomed. Among the insipidities of most Victorian verse it was the "rude inburst of air from the outside welter of human realities" needed to shock people into a recognition of the "simpleton's paradise" in which they had been living. Its characters wrestled with circumstance and passion in the sharp, truthful outlines of living human beings and not in the decoration of Arthurian dress-coats. In vividness, variety, vigor, fullness of portrayal, it was Shakespearean. Like Shakespeare, too, Browning, in confronting his readers with such a diversity of men and women and such a wide range of situations, enlarged their notions of human existence, stirred their curiosity, and expanded the play of their sympathies. He filled men, in short, with a love of humanity, and in doing that was more "powerfully efficacious from the moral point of view" than any dispenser of surface didacticism could ever be. There was no system, it must be remembered, in Plato or Shakespeare; and either one of them as a "great creative poet" probably exerted "a nobler, deeper, more permanent ethical influence than a dozen generations of professed moral teachers."

In addition to his moral strength, Browning was distinguished by the scientific attitude of his intelligence, for the whole poem was "a parable of the feeble and half-hopeless struggle which truth has to make against the ways of the world." His courageous openness of mind defended him from sterility, and, in all the play of his transforming imagination, he never lost his "resolute feeling after and grip of fact." Although there was no grandeur in *The Ring and the Book*, for which reason it was not exactly comparable to the finest of Greek plays or *Paradise Lost* or *Faust* or *Hamlet*, there was a near-equivalent: "a certain simple teaching of our sense of human kinship, of the large identity of the conditions of the human lot, of the piteous fatalities which bring the lives of the great multitude of men to be little more than grains of sand blown by the wind."

PATER

The appearance of Walter Pater's *Studies in the History of the Renaissance* was a two-fold reassurance to Morley. First, it showed him that a new school of critics might yet arise in England who would combine German thoroughness and historic sense with French acuteness and artistry of arrangement. Second, it let him see that, in spite of an objectionable preoccupation with science everywhere, there were still to be found valuable non-scientific "manifestations of intellectual activity and fruitfulness." In reviewing the work in *The Fortnightly* in 1873, characteristically not content with those aspects of Pater's work ordinarily admired, he searched for matter which could be related to the large general facts of the times. To be sure, he showed himself sensitive to the style of Pater with its "flavour at once full and exquisite" and its "infinite subtlety," and he was relieved that Pater's artistic sense and his "clear, vigorous, and ordered thought" would prevent it from falling into the particular degradation to which it is liable—"bastard dithyramb." Moreover, he praised Pater's "love of minor tones," his suggestiveness, his evocative impressionism. But what was especially significant about the substance of the criticism in the *Studies* was that it was concrete, not metaphysical; "a record or suggestion of impressions, not an analysis of their ultimate composition, nor an abstract search for the law of their effects," it was devoid of the pretentious display of "speculative and technical apparatus" that stigmatized most contemporary English art criticism and dissociated it so deplorably from life. For it was Pater's special value that he linked art with real life, that he interpreted imaginatively the significance of art in association with "human culture and the perplexities of human destiny." He was not an interferer with morals, major or minor, but cared scrupulously only to communicate the importance of "the accentuating portion of life." The growing aesthetic vogue, of which he was the most sensitive spokesman, gave promise of being a wholesome benefit to England for it disclosed that, in the midst of the bleakness and ugliness of industrialization, there existed a craving for things harmonious and beautiful.

In addition to all the essays and reviews proper there are numerous comments on English authors scattered through Morley's biographical studies and published addresses. Although these obviously do not throw any more light on his method or his temper, as gratuitous opinions and reflections, some of them are worth noticing.

It is hard to understand why he never developed a statement of his appreciation of Shakespeare, for he could have written suggestively about many of the plays. The comedies illustrated the art of "perfect fooling," in which Shakespeare, along with Rabelais and Aristophanes, was consummate; and irresistible were "the reckless buffoonery" of many of the scenes in the first part of *Henry IV* and "the mad extravagances of the Merry Wives." About *Measure for Measure*, which appealed strongly to him, his "favorite proposition" was one that not many people have come to hold even today: the play was "one of the most modern" of all of Shakespeare's, with "the profound analysis of Angelo and his moral catastrophe, the strange figure of the duke, the deep irony of our modern time in it all." He once mentioned this to Gladstone, but upon getting no response, deduced that the prime minister was "too healthy, too objective, too simple, for all the complexities of modern morbid analysis." Swift, he ranked near Voltaire as a satirist and a prose master—below him only because he was "often truculent and often brutally gross, both in thought and in phrase." Among contemporaries, Newman was distinguished by his graceful, "siren" style; the Cardinal wrote "well, divinely well." Tennyson, mentioned perhaps more often than any other contemporary poet, had a talent for exquisite music in verse which was unsurpassed, but he was occasionally illogical in his thought, as in the implications of "Maud," and, on the whole, had "hardly shown that the scientific ideas of an age were soluble in musical words." Disraeli, in spite of his political principles, was a writer of novels brilliant for "the spirit of whim in them, the ironic solemnity, the historical paradoxes, the fantastic glitter of dubious gems, the grace of high comedy, all in union

with a social vision that often pierced deep below the surface."
Yet if he was "a master of words, . . . he was also their slave";
nothing he ever wrote, despite some extraordinary vivacity and
fooling in *Vivian Gray*, had "sacred fire" or was a permanent
contribution to literature. Later in life, fascinated with Disraeli, Morley classified him with Cavour and Bismarck as one
of the great statesmen of the century; yet it is reported that
when he was approached by the executors of Disraeli's estate to
write a biography, he declined because he felt the "result would
not be artistic." Hardy bore Morley's particular admiration
and was a life-long friend as well. As a reader for Macmillan's
in his early days, Morley had come across Hardy's first novel,
The Poor Man and the Lady, seen potentialities in it, and
though he had rejected it, had got Hardy to come and see him
and been the "cause of his writing another and a better one,"
Under the Greenwood Tree. He always maintained that there
was a good deal of the Shakespearean in Hardy—here again
anticipating twentieth-century criticism.

What, after all is Morley's position as a critic? What lasting
contribution did he make to the literature of criticism? If
simply to recognize literary worth the moment he comes into
contact with it distinguishes a good critic from a mediocre, then
the fact that he discerned early the quality of such writers as
Meredith, George Eliot, Pater, Swinburne, Morris, and Hardy
stamps him as pre-eminent. His high honesty in research and
commitment are admirable; his refusal to undertake a form of
biography which he felt alien to his powers, and his assigning,
for example, the analysis and evaluation of Rousseau's produc-
tions in music to a friend more adequately equipped to treat
them, both testify to his conscientiousness. His breadth of mind,
his tolerance in dissociating morality from art and judging
works on their own merits apart entirely from the character of
writers' private lives, place him among the first of the moderns.

"Better Racine," he was always fond of quoting, "bad father, bad husband, bad friend, so that he wrote great plays, than Racine, good father, good husband, good friend, and a blockhead." Indeed, a supreme instance of such disinterestedness occurred in his study of Rousseau, to whose character he was damningly antipathetic, when, after being repelled in disgust by Rousseau's vicious erotic habits, he described certain of his *Dialogues* (1775-1776) as "masterpieces in the style of contemplative prose," unequalled in the whole of French literature for their "even, mellow gravity of tone," and their "sonorous plainsong." And in the "temple that commemorates human emancipation" he did not hesitate to reserve a place for Rousseau, intellectually abortive though he was, because he had, beyond any dispute, kindled "a brighter flame of moral enthusiasm" for his generation. Nevertheless, where the whole effect of a work was to incite its readers one way or another, he always took a firm stand; morality in its broadest sense, morality as the conviction that life must possess integrity and dignity, he never ceased to cherish, and he was bound, therefore, to estimate how far the attitude toward life of the writer whose book lay before him exalted or degraded such an ideal. All art he held to be experience transmuted into expression, but all parts of experience were not equally valuable and so the literary artist was to be judged for the kind of experience he wrought and the interpretation he placed on it. The ultimate question about any work was, "What was its worth for mankind?" By how much did it enrich human beings sensuously, intellectually, spiritually? How did it assist them, not only in directing their individual lives, but in harmonizing themselves with their fellows? The purely literary point of view, concerned with subtleties of form or mood or temperament or sensibility, was always to be subordinated in criticism.

There are other facts, too, which help to define his significance. His use of psychology in his analyses made him a path-finder. His advanced conception of his own function must not be forgotten either. The great effort he made as a critic to assist in shaping a literary atmosphere by which creative intellects could become impregnated was startlingly effectual in at least one case. No less a writer than Mrs. Humphry Ward, forty years after the appearance of his exhaustive indictment of the intellectual temper of his age, declared that she could "never lose the impression," which *On Compromise* "with its almost savage appeal for sincerity in word and deed" had made upon her—"an impression which had its share in *Robert Elsmere.*"

But it is for his historical sense, more than any other quality, that Morley's criticism has been acclaimed. G. P. Gooch, him-self a historian of repute, assigns his volumes on Burke to "a place among the classics of English political literature," and lists him as one of eight nineteenth-century writers who made "precious contributions to the story of intellectual develop-ment."[4] Ferdinand Brunetière in 1886 called Morley's treat-ment of Rousseau a "brilliant sketch"[5] and testified, thirteen years later, that although there were many volumes in French on Rousseau and Voltaire and Diderot, perhaps none existed equal to those by the German critics, Strauss and Rosenkranz, or to those by Morley.[6] It was not until 1890, more than twenty years after Morley had undertaken his French studies, that any Frenchman embarked on a project of similar scope and pur-pose, in which Voltaire, for example, was revealed to his own countrymen for what he was, an extraordinary assimilator with a genius for giving unforgettable expression to all the ideas of

---

[4] *History and Historians in the Nineteenth Century* (Longmans, Greene: 1913), p. 400, p. 584.

[5] "Voltaire et J. J. Rousseau," *Etudes Critiques sur l'Histoire de la Littérature Française*, III, p. 261.

[6] "La Littérature Européenne du XIX⁰ Siècle," *op. cit.*, VII, p. 285. ". . . mais peut-être pas un qui vaille ceux de Strauss, de Rosenkranz, et de M. John Morley." Morley, of course, knew the work of both Germans.

his age.[7] With his conception, then, of the chief advance in nineteenth-century criticism as "the substitution of becoming for being," and with his ability in "the synthetic method," Morley causes most of his contemporaries in his field to appear narrow. Only Leslie Stephen, in the amplitude of his historical perspective, the vigor of his mind, and the incisiveness of his style, can be compared to him.

The fact remains, however, in spite of Morley's importance to the growth of criticism, that his books are not read as they should be today. It is true that, since research is continually unearthing new facts and new sources of information, or proving old sources less reliable than they were once held to be, the authority of critical-historical volumes such as his diminishes from decade to decade as they are superseded by works more recent and "accurate." Gilbert Murray, a scholar-admirer of Morley's, holds that, with all its philosophic consistency, his criticism is not illuminating. This has overstrained the truth; much of it, even in the literary studies, is illuminating. Yet it cannot be denied that he is never imaginatively evocative as Walter Pater so often is. Though there is intellectual suggestion in abundance and broad historical relation, too, in his essay on Wordsworth, for example, it possesses no such intuitive insight, no such affinitive comment as does Pater's. To this difference, however, he would have been the first to own; the subtlety which he admired in Pater, he never pretended to in himself. Probably more attention to what he held secondary to

[7] See Brunetière's "Le Bilan de Voltaire," *Revue des Deux Mondes*, Mai, 1890.

Morley's appearances in translation deserve some mention. In 1895 a number of his *Critical Miscellanies* were translated into French by one G. Art, the volume appearing with the title *Essais Critiques* and containing an introduction by Augustin Filon (Paris, 346 pp.). In 1879 *On Compromise* was translated into German by Dr. Ludwig Haller and called *Uberzeugungstreue* (Carl Ruempler, Hannover). Morley's success as editor must not be overlooked either. At Leipzig in 1880 a German edition of his *English Men of Letters Series* (opened in 1878) was announced as in progress, the translator and editor being one L. Katscher. This same series, J. J. Jusserand acknowledges, was what inspired him to inaugurate his own series of *Les Grands Ecrivains Français* in 1887.

ideas, but what Carlyle held first and foremost, the human touches about his subjects, would have benefited his work. Would not the volumes on Diderot read better, one asks, if they revealed more of Diderot passing his days as Carlyle liked to think of him, "amid labour and recreation: questionable Literature, unquestionable Loves; eating and digesting (better or worse); in gladness and vexation of spirit, in laughter ending in sighs"? Yet here again, it must be remembered, Morley wrote as he wrote with a thorough realization of his limitations. Much as he admired Carlyle's *Life of Sterling* and praised again and again the imaginative virtuosity of his picture of the French Revolution, he knew that dramatic life-telling was not his province and never aimed to compete with Carlyle in it. He himself was a critic, not a creative artist. In his prose, too, one wants less sharp outlines and a suppler, softer texture occasionally; the impression is that he too often radiated heat rather than light. Although Meredith in 1876 considered his near "the finest of historical styles," and although through his last years he shared with Hardy the deanship of English letters, only four years after his death ex-Prime Minister Asquith was of the opinion that his literary reputation had been greater than he had deserved and had not withstood "the ravages of time." Undoubtedly his volumes raised what he called "the temperature of thought" of his own times, but to a generation removed from the special circumstances surrounding the issues over which he fought, many of his once strongest passages are likely to read dangerously like declamation.

The judgment, however, that Morley's prose at its best, in the French studies and the critical essays, is liturgically grandiloquent, and that grandiloquence today is out of fashion, is not enough to vindicate the neglect into which his work has fallen. The character of contemporary prose is equally alien to the styles of Macaulay, Carlyle, Newman, Ruskin, and Stevenson. His vocabulary, his syntax, and his tone are not finally the facts by which he is to be weighed. Since he was a critic, it is by his body of thought that he must stand or fall, and it is exactly this body of thought which exhibits such startling pertinency to our own day and relates him more closely, perhaps, than any of the other Victorians to the twentieth century. Ceaselessly aware that his age was one of science, industrialization, and democracy, he demanded that all writers possess such an awareness and disclose in their work a blood relationship with the times out of which they sprang. How were science, industrialization, and democracy affecting man's lot? How altering his physical state? How impinging on his ideals? What relation did they bear to the forces of pain and evil in the world? It is in his apprehensive preoccupation with these questions and in his fearful answers to them that he stands out, in part as an embodiment of, and in part a warning against, what such an eminent contemporary thinker as Mr. Joseph Wood Krutch in 1929 so searchingly diagnosed as the modern temper. That this is no haphazard observation, numerous points of contact confirm. Sixty years before Krutch's exposition, Morley had reached "The Disillusion with the Laboratory" and, in fear of it, embarked on his campaign to warn other people against its excessive pretensions. Although Thomas Huxley may have believed, as Krutch asserts, that "the superstructure of Christian morality would stand after the supernatural props" had been knocked out from underneath, Morley did not; for fifty years he lamented that no ethics could remain sound "on the shifting sands and rotting foundations of theology" and strove to develop some other kind of social belief which would sustain them. As for "Love—or the Life and Death of a Value," he had warned, in discussing Diderot in 1878, that the deeper "unsparing and unblushing" science probed into the phenomenon, the more miserable men and women would be; to strip sexual attraction of its centuries-old moral associations would be to "return to the nakedness of the brute," a catastrophic retrogression. With regard to "The Tragic Fallacy," his discussion of Victor Hugo in 1874 had pointed out that for modern man tragedy could no longer inhere in the grand yet unrealizable Destiny of the ancient Greeks but must be faced as the scientific product of cause and effect, of "the resistless compulsion of circumstance . . . invariable antecedent and invariable consequent." His unflinching courage in the face of this realization was somewhat at variance, however, with what Krutch depicts as the self-torturing inertia which seizes many disillusioned contemporaries. Sighing in his quest of Truth on the steep, tortuous paths over which she led him, Morley knew well the elusiveness of Krutch's "Phantom of Certitude"; no less sensitive to "The Paradox of Humanism," he, too, had determined that he would rather die as a man than live as an animal.

CHAPTER FIVE

Private Life and Last Years
A Comparison and a Summary

I

THE last nine years of Morley's life gave him an opportunity to savor uninterrupted what he had been so careful
to preserve through his long public career, the precious "delicacy and bloom" of life. Once in his youth he had written that
these qualities were unattainable through living simply, because simplicity was at best a negative virtue; but what he
termed simplicity, one discovers by an observation of his mature domestic and social habits, might better have been called
parsimony. The tranquillity, the cool quietness, the immacu-
lateness, the restful, discreet whiteness which so attracted an
admiring French visitor in 1891 remained distinctions of his
household to the end. His wants were never multiplied; his
tastes, never complicated. Refinement was hyper-discriminat-
ing, rarefied, in him; among the increasing distractions of a
mechanical age he could not endure that the constituents of
his routine should become dominating absorptions. He desired
comfort but never coveted a large "establishment." He kept no
butler, never owned an automobile, and spoke with amused
self-depreciation about "We middle-class people disguised as
Peers." Most important in his ordered, serene domesticity were
his books, his confessed "genial, instructive, fortifying com-
rades," and his wife. About the exact character of her place in
his scheme of things there can be only conjecture, as futile as in
most cases, owing to the lack of information about her, it tends
to be suspicious. In his own words, the relations between a man
and his wife "are those of which even the nearest friend must
know least," for success or failure in them, right or wrong

about them, are dependent on "elements too delicate to be capable of being either fully divulged or fairly seized." Who can gainsay him? He took no delight in prying open cupboard doors on other men's skeletons, and so in his own marital life merits the consideration of *de mortuis nil nisi bonum*. Rose Ayling, whom he married in 1870, was a sweetly charming girl, a cyclist, a walker, a country-lover, who, in spite of not being a philosophic conversationalist or a cosmopolitan winer-and-diner, could talk interestingly with John Stuart Mill in his last years about flowers and birds, and elicit the affection of her husband's oldest friends. Certainly the note of assurance later on in Morley's line to his warm French friend J. J. Jusserand on the subject of Jusserand's approaching marriage—"This, I trust, is to prove the happiest event of your life"—indicates nothing but happy compatibility in his own home.

Outside his house, music and friendly companionship remained inexhaustible delights. Morley, who, as a youth could hardly tolerate going to St. John's for Good Friday services "because there was no organ," continued partial to organ music and "reveled" in it for an hour every morning when he visited at Skibo, the Scottish estate of his American friend, Andrew Carnegie. The frequency with which he was seen in churches satisfying his love of liturgical music gave rise to the rumor that he was about to turn Catholic, in refutation of which he had to assure his friends that he would as soon turn Negro. His social intercourse, however, the war temporarily interrupted. He withdrew from the Cabinet in 1914 convinced that Hell was raging on earth and men had gone mad, and his resentment, his deep indignation led him for a time to be brusque and stern in his answers to letters of sympathy from those devoted to him; he seemed to have severed all ties with the past. But gradually he returned to the world, and with him his historical sense, his eagerness over international events, his affection, and his charm. For it was charm. His personal relationships had all along been distinguished by inimitable grace and warm sincerity, and numerous testimonies have been made by men and women who were enriched by his company. Indeed, once at a party when the guests decided to write on slips of paper the name of the man they would prefer to have as companion on a desert island, the choice was unanimous for Morley! Even in the give-and-take of politics, the effect of his personality was unmistakable. When a bystander remarked to a young Scotch conservative, fresh from a talk with Morley, that he seemed to get on well with the English politician, the answer came back: "If all Radicals were like Morley they would be easy to get on with—and perhaps there would be fewer conservatives." It was true, as Mrs. Humphry Ward was later to attest, that Morley knew "all through his life what it was to be courted, by men and women alike, for the mere pleasure of his company." He was captivating, and the impression he made, instantaneous and enduring. In addition to the high moral atmosphere in which he moved, he possessed a "singular personal power," an inexplicable magic which winged his words and gave them force. He had succeeded, as he early set out to do, in capturing "the genuine air and manner of distinction."

In his old age Morley's connoisseurship in wines and foods was something for younger men to marvel at and profit by; yet he was as fastidious in his affections as in his tastes and delighted in relating one with the other. Said one of the protégés who profited:

He would be there a quarter of an hour before the time carefully choosing from the menu and ordering the wine. Often his greeting would be: "You're a red-wine man, and I remember that you liked that Margaux, and see, I have got it again." It was delightfully flattering and ever so kind.[1]

[1] J. A. Spender, "Lord Morley, Last of Victorian Liberals," *Living Age*, CCCXIX (November, 1923).

But it was in his conversation that his charm was supreme. In no other aspect of his social behavior was he so much the artist. If his mere presence cast the spell, it was his speech that sealed and sustained it. A three-hours' talk with him was an unforgettably happy experience, and you knew, once you had shared in one, that to be banned from his company was a genuine bereavement. It was exactly the quiet, easy flow he had early cultivated in his conversation that set him apart from other men, enlivened as it was now and then by "pungent bits of absurdity," but never conspicuously pointed by flashy paradoxes or strained by disputatiousness. His voice was soft, courteous, urbane, yet tinged sometimes with delicate irony or almost imperceptible superciliousness. And so deferential was he, so intent on avoiding wrangling that he became more and more accustomed to yielding point after point, fact after fact, to his companions. Yet it was not deference alone which prompted him thus. It was as much true Socratic humility; when he saw truth in an idea, he was compelled to concede it. Arguing for truth rather than victory, often he went so far in his concessions that there was no retracing—nothing to do but throw up his hands with an "Ah!" and let the subject disappointingly drop.[2] Frequently his silence and willingness to listen worked an unintentional deception on men who were overeager to persuade him; what was patient, receptive disinterestedness, they were too ready to construe as tacit acquiescence. Indeed, not all who talked with Morley found him wholly satisfying. His life-long fondness for freshly phrased commonplaces or aphoristic quotations, some companions thought handicapping. What he called his "elegant extracts," chosen from the vast stores of his

---

[2] Austin Harrison, in his *Frederic Harrison: Thoughts and Memories*, describes the long discussions between his father and Morley. Morley, he says, remained "dissolvent and dubious," while Harrison, who generally won, soared pontifically, "all contention, a *sabreur* in thought." "Lord Morley was economic with adjectives and constitutionally chary of generalizations. His brow would dome and his lips curl. 'Well! Well!,' he would say, 'I envy you your turmoil. You are like a tankard of old sack.'"

commonplace books, were habitually intruding upon his own thoughts, breaking their flow, and, while they often imparted a brilliant coloring, they were sometimes likely to convey the impression of a man walking on crutches rather than his own legs.

During the latter part of his political life, although he was not a party leader, Morley relished playing Nestor to his colleagues. Year after year he gave a dinner at Elm Park Gardens just before the opening of Parliament, at which, in Prime-Minister Asquith's words, he "entertained and admonished his younger and more mutinous friends." After his withdrawal from politics, he was content to be the Nestor of journalism. At one time or another all rising journalists of any account sought counsel from him—it was the "first rule of the game in the eighties and nineties." As long as he lived, he was proud of his own journalistic past and both curious and eager to know what progress the press was making in other countries; a question about it was among the first things he asked of visitors from abroad.

His interest in politics remained avid to the end; and there was no flagging in his zeal for fame or his attachment to the "secondary adjuncts" of place and ceremony.[3] In the long months of strife between England and Ireland in 1921, he looked back regretfully on the failure of his own efforts to bring about Home Rule more than a quarter of a century before. At one point, after the rejection by the House of Lords of a new bill for Irish independence, he confessed in agitation to a friend, "I should like to have been there if only to have got up and said, 'If Mr. G.'s Home Rule Bill had been passed thirty years ago could Ireland have been worse than it is now? Would it not have been better?'—And then fallen dead like Lord

---

[3] It has been said that when Sir Henry Campbell-Bannerman was forming his Liberal government in 1905, "Morley applied to be appointed to every post in the Cabinet, except that of Prime Minister," and "it was with a feeling of being ill-used that he subsided with a coronet into the Secretaryship of State for India"! See "Morley's Fears for his Life," *The Literary Digest*, LXXX (January 12, 1924).

Chatham."[4] On December 16, 1921, when peace between England and Ireland was finally reached and a treaty signed, Morley had his last moment of public glory. Supported by his nephew, he went down into the House of Lords, and tottering slightly and in a cracked voice which, pathetically, could not be heard more than a few feet away, placed his benediction upon the measure. He had lived to see the consummation of the old dream, and true to his pledge had never forsaken the cause.

Morley's last days were days of gradual euthanasia. Gout, growing deafness, weakness of memory had all been the first symptoms of a general decline. He spent much time in a chair with one of his books always in his lap, for moving from room to room, even with the support he had to have, was too great a strain for his worn frame. He did little reading, however; scrutiny of his face revealed his eyes to be looking not at the words on the page before him but through them to the invisible past beyond. He spent many of his waking hours in reminiscent reverie, always with quiet, gentle satisfaction, for the lines around his mouth were relaxed and the frailest shade of a smile lightened his lips. Outside of retrospection, his thoughts were much on death, to which he resigned himself with tranquil patience, and he would read aloud the passage from Dante's *Convito*, where death is compared to the haven which the soul, like a battered mariner, reaches after all struggle is past. What he had set himself forty years earlier to avoid, there was becomingly not a trace of—"those unmanly repinings or any of that garrulous self-pity which not seldom, even in the case of men who have done good work in their noontide, rob the close of life of its becoming dignity and fortitude." His "large and serene internal activity" protected him to the end.[5]

---

[4] J. H. Morgan, "The Personality of Lord Morley," *Quarterly Review*, CCXLI (January, 1924).

[5] According to J. H. Morgan, Morley, as a result of his life-long respect for thrift, left a fortune of some sixty thousand pounds, the bulk of it the product of his literary life, prudently invested by a friend.

II

Morley's last twenty-five years found him preoccupied with the old antiphonal, equivocal questioning themes. Human nature—was it good or bad? Which was superior, the man of letters or the man of action? What were the bounds between public and private morality? To be sure, experience modifies and moderates any man's ideas, and the radicalisms of today are the platitudes of tomorrow. But even so, Morley's intellectual life is not one to be graphed by an even, regular curve from left to right. His mental equipoise was never destroyed; the balance in his philosophic comprehension, never broken. Unfortunately, the war and its aftermath tinged his tone with bitterness, with something, at times, of hopelessness; and so the effect of that cataclysm, wholly out of proportion to anything else, must always be taken into account in surveying the field of his aged mind. Still, what remains remarkable is the consistency of his opinions.

The man of letters, he had decided at twenty-five, is always inferior to the man of action, and to his death he maintained that decision. No number of publisher's royalties could swerve him from preferring the indescribable satisfaction of saying "Yea" or "Nay" in vital questions of state to "the solitude, the nervous exhaustion, the introspection of the life" of writing. This, contradictorily, from the man whose conscience in politics had worried him into writing innumerable letters of resignation! The truth is that he took pleasure in endlessly debating the balance between the two professions; although he had exalted politics above literature, he never, for that reason, for-

---

With his characteristic aversion to biographical exploration, he was explicit in his will about his collected papers. He sent all his "correspondence, diaries, and written fragments" to his nephew, Guy Estell Morley, "to be dealt with as he may think fit at his own discretion." His executors were enjoined "to refuse to aid and encourage" anybody in writing a biography of him, "and not to allow any such person to have access to any of" his "papers, whether personal or acquired in the course of official duty, either for perusal or otherwise."

sook literature. A "favorite catechism" of his was, which, if one had had his choice, would one rather have been, Gibbon or Pitt, Macaulay or Palmerston? and his remembrance of the pleasure of writing was so keen that until he was incapacitated, he toyed periodically with the notion of doing biographical studies of Cavour, Disraeli, Strafford, Calvin, Lucretius, and Goethe! His young friend Gilbert Murray tried to draw him back to exercising his pen, but the pull was not strong enough; yet when Thomas Hardy remarked that if only he "had let politics alone, he might have been the Gibbon of his age," he was "visibly disquieted." His persistence in attempting to embrace a duality of achievement was discomforting; he was once heard expressing the wish that he could "walk along the House of Lords with Aristotle on one arm and Machiavelli on the other." It is true that, much as he condemned Machiavellianism, he was irresistibly attracted to men of blood and iron and relished being in their company. The pleasure he experienced in the vivacity of Kaiser Wilhelm, on the few occasions when he was with the German monarch, is at least ingenuous.[6]

"In a moral aspect," Morley had written in 1867, "the fineness of the material of which a friend's character is made, is surely far more important to me, than the correctness of his intellectual impressions." Throughout the *Fortnightly* epoch it was because he believed this so firmly that he preached the need of more history in schools to offset the exclusive emphasis on science; history, properly studied, would enrich character and instill beneficence. Even in introducing the French Encyclopedists to England, he was periodically careful to guard his readers against the falsehood that physical science alone could improve the lot of man. And in 1911 at seventy-three, with the eloquence of anxiety, he exhorted students at the University of Manchester to shun that "exaggerated and misshapen rational-

[6] See, for expressions of his pleasure, *Recollections*, I, p. 247, and II, p. 199 and p. 298.

ism that shuts out imagination, distrusts sentiment, despises tradition." Certainly no man's life could have been a more noble illustration of his convictions on such a question than was his own, with its sympathy and benignance.

About the effect of science on literature he had been deeply concerned for several decades. In 1873 he had on the whole welcomed it for the increased seriousness and thoroughness in which it would result. As the years went on, however, an apprehension formed: "Is the pure scientific impulse—to tell the truth with all the necessary reservations—easy to combine with regard for artistic pleasure?" In his old age he himself answered the question, chiefly in the negative: although science had developed the desire for truth in men and taught them to be patient in their quest of it, in prose style it had led to increasing complexity, on the historian it had imposed a tremendous burden of documentation, and in fiction it had given rise to an ominous vogue for bold, unsparing analysis.

Along with Morley's reasoned depreciation of science and intellect, lasted his preference for the company of churchmen. The older he grew, the more fully he exemplified the truth in his dictum, "It is certainly not less possible to disbelieve religiously than to believe religiously." Christian morality, he had always counseled and tried to practice; but more than this he had always aspired to, and in his old age reflected, that exalted, sublimated state of soul called "holiness." This was an "inner grace of nature" by which man's spirit was to commune with the "seen and the unseen Good," a "deep feeling for things of the spirit that are unknown and incommensurable, a sense of awe, mystery, sublimity," the equivalent, perhaps, of Matthew Arnold's special kind of emotion by which morality was to be touched. He knew well the agitation of beauty such as one feels in Shelley's "Skylark" "or a piece of ineffable, heart-searching melody by Beethoven or Handel," and he could be appropriately reverent in the presence of it. Once, as a guest in

Ireland of the Countess of Aberdeen, although he had been considerately excused by his hostess from participating in them, he insisted on joining family prayers every morning "to renew his own sense of littleness amid the mysteries of life, and to begin the day with a feeling of fellowship in service with the humblest member of the household." Again in Scotland, where his host was a Highlander, he surprised and delighted other guests by standing with them at the piano on Sunday evenings and singing hymns as heartily as anyone in the company. Upon the death of his friend Herbert Spencer in 1903 he was asked to employ his prestige to obtain a burial in Westminster Abbey, but he refused, for his knowledge of Spencer's atheism left him unable to view such an interment as anything but an act of desecration. On one of the last trips he ever made to Rome, he left the train specifically to see two men and two men only— the Pope and the Vicar-General of the Jesuits! Neither one was accessible, and in disappointment, unobserved, he made his departure.

The nature and limits of compromise never ceased to concern Morley. Where must frankness leave off and reticence begin? In the preparatory *Saturday Review* days he had decried unremitting, extreme self-assertion. Tact was not to be identified with hypocrisy; and a certain willingness to hear other people's opinions, in spite of a burning itch to controvert them, was imperative if the world was to be preserved from degenerating into a "sheer bear garden." All that he, as a Utilitarian, could say in behalf of the relentless self-speaker was that, although his habit of continually quarreling with whatever his neighbors did and thought was "fully as objectionable as a habit of mentally bowing and scraping before them," it was "probably not so bad for the man himself." The famous *On Compromise* (1874), his fullest exposition of his opinions on the subject, explained in detail how the bear garden could be avoided. It commanded men to allow their minds no compromise with strict truth, to be merciless to themselves in their search for it, no matter how discomforting the results might be. At the same time it advocated a considerate restraining of tongues in company with others. On points of belief, in all matters of individual conscience, any evasion or misrepresentation of facts was insupportable, but in the proprieties of social intercourse, to escape the antagonizing ferment which ruthless frankness in small matters would create, a discreet skirting of argumentative declarations was necessary. In the patient gentleness of Morley's old age, nothing was further removed from his speech than promiscuous and universal sneering. No man could have practiced better the gracefulness he preached.

To what extent were principles of individual conduct reconcilable with public life? Were the bounds of private and public morality the same? In 1867, impatient idealist though he was, Morley knew that to hold public office one had to compromise, to conciliate, to struggle, to submit to defeat. But at the same time he could not refrain from asking the question:

Have moral considerations, again, any place in political transactions; or are we to learn that though it is atrocious for a man to cheat, lie, and murder for his personal profit, these actions become harmless or even laudable when they are committed for the benefit of a government or a corporation?

Because he vigorously denied through his *Fortnightly* association that immorality and inhumanity on the part of the state could be vindicated, he condemned English imperialism. As a politician, however, he learned that some modifications of the Christian code were inescapable; politics began for him as simply common sense, they changed intermediately to "a rough second best," and they ended as "a matter of expediencies." He would not pose as an exemplar and developed a strong dislike for the nickname coined for him, "Honest John." In his old age he confessed that public morality had to be separate from private, and admitted that he had never known a Cabinet meeting where anyone had discussed a question as a Christian, not even Gladstone himself. Still, a second best in political morality was better than no best at all, and after more than thirty years of unrest in trying to adjust his conscience to it, he refused to yield to an additional lowering of standards from second to third. His Cabinet resignation spared him further, deeper pain.

In the genuineness of his attitude toward labor, however, and in the clarity of his thoughts on panaceas, Morley remained "Honest John" to his death. As *Fortnightly* editor he had never patronized workmen, never simulated fraternity for them, never talked as one of them. His bearing in front of them had always been one of man-to-man respect, of sympathetic understanding. In his decline he was no less straightforward. Labor intellectuals, more and more in fashion, he despised. And not for a minute did he lose sight of what constituted real gains, real improvements for those who worked. When it was pointed out to him what increases in wages, what reductions in hours, what multiplication of conveniences the twentieth century had brought "the masses," he asked anxiously and somewhat sharply whether they were better men and women than they had been; so far as he could see, they cared no more for things of the mind, for husbands only squandered their money on betting, wives on "meretricious finery." For panaceas he retained characteristically little regard. Even democracy, he persisted in reminding people, using a phrase of the Archbishop of York's of which he was fond, even democracy has no divine right. About Socialism he never altered his skepticism; he would make no stronger statement for it than that he delivered in 1911, that it was "still a secret" whether, "in any of its multitudinous forms," it could be "the assured key to progress." To the end he maintained that the survival of civilization depended on a readjusting of the scales for a harmonious, equitable balance between individual initiative on the one

hand and state control on the other. As for the Covenant of
the League of Nations, he dismissed it, in spite of his deep-
rooted anti-militarism, with withering contempt. What would
a scrap of paper do by way of keeping the world from war?
There would be no peace until there were ministers in all countries bent on peace. Did he recollect at all his own plan, advanced almost fifty years before, for a league of powers to
maintain peace, led by England and so constituted as to enforce
diplomatic decisions by economic and military sanctions?

The debacle of the war and the folly of the Versailles settlement led to serious doubts about the nature of man and ominous conjectures about his future. Were human beings, after
all, bad? Was his life-long assurance that they could be taught
to be good, proven false at last? In the late 1890's, alarmed by
the unchecked growth of "the turbid whirlpools of a military
age," he had re-examined the whole ground of human character and human history. In his essay "Machiavelli," he had
vindicated men and judged the Italian's view of things un-
sound; Machiavelli possessed intellectual strength but he was
short-sighted because he lacked "moral grandeur." The growth
of the Machiavellian spirit among nations in modern times
could be explained even though there was no inherent rightness
in the philosophy underlying it; what made it so fearfully
prevalent was that "Science, with its survival of the fittest" was
unconsciously lending it "illegitimate aid." Machiavellianism
could be interpreted, then, as natural "energy, force, will, violence," which are hostile to man unless harnessed and controlled. It was not at all a figment to be laughed away but a
power at large in the universe, against which civilized men and
women everywhere must be ceaselessly on guard. In his "Guicciardini," soon after, Morley was relieved to be able to quote
another Italian historian, who, he said, had given a truer view
of the case. According to Guicciardini, men are not naturally
bad but only naturally weak, so that even when they incline

toward the good, their frailty, aggravated by worldly distractions, prevents them from doing what they have set out to do. At least this way of looking at human nature left room for hope: worldly distractions from virtue might still be transformed into worldly inducements toward it, and human reason and will strengthened through education. And so, as late as 1908, Morley denied any truth in Carlyle's Machiavellian verdict: that "the ultimate question between any two human beings is—Can I kill thee, or canst thou kill me?" Shaken, however, by the desperate plight of the world after 1918, by the mockery of what was termed peace, and in a siege of despondency, he exclaimed to a friend that "to the end of time" it would "always be a case of 'Thy head or my head.' "[7]

What of progress through the long range of centuries? Had civilization advanced or retrogressed? Never one to desire an immediate and faultless millennium or to believe in a progress that was automatous, though, to be sure, his tone in speaking of it had at one time not invariably been temperate, Morley gazed wonderingly, somewhat quizzically at the great notion in 1904. He was unable to define it, but, since he had recently read in an American book a story about a father who had wanted fifteen things, got ten, and worried about five, whereas his son wanted forty, got thirty, and worried more about the ten remaining, he was willing to suggest that "one clause in any definition of advance in civilization might be that progress lies in the constant increase in the number of things wanted, in the number of those who want them, and the greater worry if the things wanted are not got."[8] From that time on it was his habit to describe a belief in the certainty of progress as a superstition, a radiant but delusive fatalism. In 1911, as Chancellor of the University

---

[7] J. H. Morgan, "The Personality of Lord Morley." F. W. Hirst, however, in his preface to *The Early Life and Letters*, prints a very late commitment to the effect that Carlyle's pronouncement put "the case too bluntly"; it was "only an extreme form of mercantile competition."

[8] "Some Thoughts on Progress," *Educational Review*, XXIX (January, 1905).

of Manchester, he was perturbed and dubious: the track, he urged his students to see, was not all upward; progress was an "eternal riddle" with its meaning "extremely diverse"; and he confessed that he was "content with something far short of Mill's assumption" that there was at least "great progress in feelings and opinions." In 1919, in a moment of depression, he could only ask tragically, "As for progress, what signs of it are there now? And all we Victorians believed in it from the Utilitarians onwards."

This darkening skepticism cast its clouds inevitably over his attitude toward history and toward literature in general. In 1913, before the storm of the war had broken, he could still celebrate history, in his accustomed way, as the queen of all studies. "It is history that matters," he told the members of the Historical Congress at Oxford, "It is history that matters more than logic, [it is] forces, incident, and the long tale of consummating circumstances." And he could go on to contrast the historian, who, like a bird, soars aloft over mountain ranges and sees that all the peaks are not of the same chain, with the politician, who, like a sailor, moves along the base, and to the side, of the same towering masses and fancies them all interconnected. Only a year before he died, however, he was lamenting that the truth could never be known and maintaining that history was always misleading because "far more depended on the conversations of half an hour, and was transacted by them than ever appeared in letters and dispatches." Deprecatingly, he called his own attempts at history "all the greater reason why he should sin no more." All his life, moreover, he had abhorred and warned against vulgar style and cheap taste in literature; yet the older he grew, the more alarmed he became by the observation that more and more the vulgar style was the democratized style and the cheap, sordid taste the democratized taste. Newspaper standards were accepted as final criteria, and the force of a "defiling flood of hideous trans-Atlantic vulgarisms" was carrying everything before it. Slang and sensationalism ruled the day. Fiction, in particular, taking its cue from French models, was being degraded; writers were wallowing in mud for its own sake. Once on a train to Calais he had found two French novels so disgusting that he had flung them out of the window. Everywhere brutalizations of the literary ideal! Democratizing books, teaching all people to read, was entirely different from democratizing writing, allowing anybody to become an author; that, he had always held. Yet he was discovering that everywhere the urge to write was following the experience of having read. Had he not sinned then, in helping to make the satisfaction of that urge possible? His ground for his conduct as a Liberal all along had been that, for things aesthetic and moral as well as for things political, he had faith in human intelligence, in the power of "a grand reserve of wise, thoughtful, unselfish, longsighted men and women" to raise standards in larger areas around itself. Was it to be true, on the contrary, that the leavening power of an intelligent minority would dissipate itself and the few succumb to the lower level of the many? Had he been wrong all the time in estimating the capacities of human beings and in considering a democratic system most beneficial to those capacities? Were discipline, taste, and ideals in all activities to be thrown to the winds? Whether he was mistaken, time and changing circumstance have not yet shown. What must be admitted about him, and remembered, is the great truth he had laid down in his youth about Burke, that the next best thing to being right with humanity and breadth is being wrong with humanity and breadth.

Despite attacks of perplexity and dejection, Morley was not engulfed by despair in his last five years. The breadth and equal-voicedness of his brain sustained him. Although to one young friend at one time he alleged that he would no longer tell electors "how to think," because he believed "in the regiments of parties" and disliked "that hateful heresy, proportional representation," to another disciple on another occasion very late in life he recalled that what had lifted England from the post-Napoleonic morass was Benthamite-Cobdenian liberality and suggested that a reintroduction of something like it into human activity might prove a salvation again. And in his personal life he remained resolute in affirming that life was worth living. He had walked with a stalwart stride, seen his share of the deeds of men, and reconciled himself in his decay, as he had early learned he must do, to the way of Nature. There was no corrosive peevishness, no self-pity, no sullen complaining, no loud-mouthed railing against humanity. What for a while, under the shock of the war, was a silent, smouldering, resentful defiance became at last a mellowed, stoical resignation, a high-minded Lucretian serenity. His own share of noxious elements did not overtake him until the end, yet even then his thankfulness for a life-long freedom from them enabled him to confront them with dignity, to yield to them with the inner grace of holiness. For his bearing, testified one who was near to him in the final days, was Christlike, and the "essential quality of his soul . . . loving-kindness."

Only a week or so before his death, Morley was asked whether consistency was a valuable virtue in politics. He didn't think much of it, he replied, and then, in answer to a question asking why he had practiced it for so long, said calmly, to save himself trouble. In spite of his disparagement, however, the truth is that one distinction of his life is the consistency of it all—consistency not only in the single threads of his thought but in the double strands as well. Was it not this very philosophic equivocalness of mind, this intellectual disposition to see both sides of an argument and weigh them heavily and long, which accounted for his moderation, his equity, his patience, and his sympathy? But though it saved him from fanaticism, was it not this trait which kept him from political leadership?

He knew indeed with Pascal what it was to seek truth with many a sigh.

III

Joseph Chamberlain, Morley once said, had a genius for friendship. The remark is no less applicable to himself. Just as he had written some of his most eloquent paragraphs on the subject in his youth, so through the rest of his life he lived that eloquence. He was as susceptible as Henry James to "demonstrations of regard," but he took no more pleasure in receiving than in bestowing esteem. He had a deep capacity for affection, of which, never prodigal, he gave unstintingly to those of whom he was fond. One reason why he was so successful in preserving his long chain of friendships was that he never debased the ideal, never feigned devotion or intimacy, or prostituted them once they existed, for political advancement. His personal life, he kept independent from his public, and inviolable by it; the encircling tides and currents of petty intrigue never sucked him in. He was not one to give parties to buy over high-priced opponents, not one to play bridge or golf to ingratiate himself among his enemies. Furthermore, knowing friendship to be an art, he had early measured the degree to which mastery of it depended upon awareness and refinement of subtle intuitive communication between temperaments. Rationalist though he was, he was sensitive to affinities, respectful of them; for him always the essence and solace of friendship resided in a "consciousness of an occult sympathy" and he never ceased to cherish, Aladdin-like, the glowing "air of magic" that surrounded the responsive play of personalities.

Both in the number and quality of his attachments Morley was extraordinary. Among nineteenth-century English writers, he numbered as special and life-long intimates, Harrison, Stephen, Meredith, Arnold, and Hardy; among contemporary British statesmen, Chamberlain, Harcourt, Roseberry, and Asquith; among foreign statesmen and writers, Mazzini, Clémenceau, Taine, and Jusserand; among American men of note, E. L. Godkin, C. E. Norton, and Andrew Carnegie. Statements survive in their letters or biographies bearing witness to the depth of the bond that bound them to him. In Meredith's correspondence the most unreserved and most poignant expressions of affection are those addressed to Morley. He made no secret of it: he loved Morley, who was a "great delight" to him, and he was rejoiced and refreshed by seeing him. When his wife died it was Morley alone who was asked to her funeral to back him on his "forlorn march of dust."[9] Leslie Stephen was no less explicit in his avowals. Morley was one of two with whom he could "be sure of finding thorough sympathy" in conversation; there was no other friend in England whom it gave him "such pleasure to meet." And after the tragic death of his first wife, he assured Morley that he would remember him thenceforth "as a man who has been through a cruel operation would remember the kind friend who stood by and spoke words of encouragement and affection." The relations between Morley and Prime-Minister Asquith were so close that, at the time of the outbreak of the World War, in answer to Asquith's repeated appeal to withdraw his resignation and retain his place in the Cabinet, Morley, in anguish over the impossibility of continuing his loyalty to his friend and obeying his conscience, wrote, "I am more distressed in making this reply than I have ever been in writing any letter of all my life." And Asquith did not hesitate to declare that Morley's death meant "the disappearance of the last survivor of a heroic age," though his knowledge of Morley's character led him to admit that literature was more impoverished than politics by his loss; he always lamented

[9] According to R. E. Sencourt (*The Life of George Meredith*, New York, Scribner's, 1929, Preface, p. ix), Morley, as one of the trustees of Meredith's estate, applied in vain after his death to Sir James Barrie to be allowed to write a biography of him.

that Morley had not remained what by temperament and intellect he was meant to be, a man of letters.

J. J. Jusserand, French diplomat and literary historian, at the end of his life could look back so appreciatively on his years of warm association with Morley that he termed him wholeheartedly "one of the best friends I made along the path of life." In 1904, as Ambassador to the United States, he had relished Morley's warning him in Washington that, when the Liberals won the coming election in England, he would have himself appointed Foreign Secretary in order to declare war against France if Jusserand was not sent Ambassador to London. And in 1917 he had been stirred by a reminiscent letter from Morley: "It would be sorrow indeed for me to leave the world without being followed by your good will, that has so long been one of the prizes of my days. Let me remain, in spite of my negligence of a rather distracted life, your affectionate friend."

E. L. Godkin in 1867 found Morley, on his brief visit to America, "a very sensible and good fellow, though not hilarious," and "liked him very much." When he learned that Morley would probably not see "anybody in Boston of any particular value," he wrote him a letter of introduction to Charles Eliot Norton there. Both meetings ripened into lasting friendships. When Godkin was in London in 1889, he rejoiced at seeing again, after twenty-two years, "the good, delightful, wholly-satisfactory John Morley"; and Norton, who later, when he, too, was in London in 1872 and 1900, saw much of Morley and agreed with him "in belief and opinion . . . more nearly than with most men" because he was "eminently sincere, and clear-minded" and free from "narrow hard-and-fastness," was fortified by Morley's brief return to Boston in 1904, even though the two got to see each other only once, because it proved to him that after almost forty years, their "old friendship remained firm." The attachment between Morley and Andrew Carnegie, though it was formed later than either of those with the other two eminent Americans, developed more strongly and revealed more strikingly certain of the essential, actuating sympathies within Morley himself. For was not Carnegie, if not a man of letters, at least an author in his own right, with his social and political essays, his industrial and economic analyses, and his biography of James Watt? More than that, was he not a man of action, a builder, a doer, a power-wielder? Morley's admiration and sentiment went out to him, in spite of the amusing fact that he had once evaluated any great capitalist, no matter how high his ability and capacities, as "below even a second-rate statesman or a second-rate general." It was not only that Carnegie had had the providence, the will, and the industry to amass a great fortune; it was that he possessed the beneficence and the understanding to distribute it wisely. And what congeniality of thought there was in him! His comprehension of true thrift, his belief that the interests of capital and labor were the same, his suspicious incredulity with regard to socialism, his staunch confidence in the workableness of democracy, his love of peace, his active international-mindedness (in particular, his interest in Anglo-American relations)—did not all of these mark him as an exemplar of the broad-minded, wide-visioned, co-operative industrial leader on whom the future depended? In 1902, in real man-of-action fashion, he showed his affection for Morley by presenting him with the sixty-odd thousand volumes of the vast personal library of the late Lord Acton, and in his will, no less characteristically, he left a testimonial to the extent of an annuity of ten thousand dollars.

Not even the firmest of Morley's friendships endured, however, without occasional tension and rupture, usually the mischief of misunderstanding. In his seriousness and responsibility to truth, he sometimes had trouble in knowing where to suspend rigorous judgment and defer to easy geniality. Chamberlain, whom he loved and whose death in 1914 left a painful void in his life, caused him many struggles with his conscience, for Chamberlain was fond of voicing the phrase "natural rights," and Morley, who, as Lord Acton wrote, would allow man no rights since he had denied God any, was thrown into as much perturbation on hearing it as if he "had seen a deinotherian shambling down Parliament Street to a seat in the House of Commons." When he and Chamberlain parted company politically over the questions of Home Rule and imperialism, his misgivings about continuing their private intimacy were so strong that it was some weeks before he could convince himself that it would be all right to accept Chamberlain's usual Christmas gift of a barrel of oysters. Frederic Harrison, too, knew how chary one had to be about trespassing on Morley's strict conscientiousness. In 1902, soon after Morley had been given his O.M., Harrison as a joke sent him a worshipful, servile letter with his title printed boldly on the envelope; he got back a sharp protest, written in unmistakable annoyance.

George Meredith, perhaps more than anyone else, felt the rebuke of Morley's fitfully severe reasonableness. This might have been expected, since in certain essentials the two were temperamentally repellent. At any rate, Morley was often irritated beyond patience by what it seemed to him Meredith's brilliant, flaring talk became—artful affectation—and left his company indignant and resentful. But if Meredith felt rebukes, he knew the happy reassurance of apology, too. Morley invariably came back, subdued, reattuned, eager to go on. Even in 1902, after a recent "delightful give and take" at dinner, Meredith could still glow at receiving a letter from him asking "to renew the past." What is significant, of course, about all these strains and breaches is not that they occurred but that they were all healed. In spite of what seemed at times a "waywardness in his disposition" to make him alternately charm and vex his friends, Morley never lost sight of the lasting and paramount value of human affection; to the end he kept himself unsullied by that gratuitous perversity which sows alienation for no reason and to no end.

IV

"No one should write his own life," Morley had decided in his middle twenties, "who cannot conscientiously invite the world in general to come and be edified." In this conviction he persisted to his death. Records of lives should exist not only to convey information but to impart encouragement through example. Human beings, in order to give their best, need to be shown that other men and women before them have lived successful, ordered lives. If they are to be disheartened at the outset by pseudo-scientific, sensationalizing records of the pigsty which at bottom every human character is supposed to be, then society may as well be abandoned. Like other intelligent men before and after him, he believed in the virtue of restraint and reticence, of discrimination and proportion.

It is with a consideration of these things that a study of his own life is edifying. In a world torn as much by the doubts of those who live within democracy as by the attacks of those who have disclaimed it, the Liberalism which he embodied, with its substance the enlightened staunchness of individual thought and character, not the slippery, hypnotic catchwords of political slogans, appears more and more a last, but a disappearing, hope. What more inept criticism of him could be made than that, in ignorance of what democracy really is, he made the mistake of refusing to identify himself with the tastes and ideals of the majority after willingly subscribing to its political judgment? To be sure, what he had written in *Edmund Burke* in 1867 about the claims of the multitude being sovereign and paramount, just because it is the multitude, he adhered to until the end. But these were claims in the political and social sphere only. The multitude never became a colossal idol before which he prostrated himself. It was endowed with common sense and he believed in its capacity for improvement, but it had to be taught and led; its ideas and tastes and moral conceptions, simply because it was the multitude, amounted to nothing. The incomparable advantage of a democracy lay in the increased number of avenues which it opened to leadership, in its greater means for producing educated, superior men and women. As a historian, he knew well the value of relativity, but that did not prevent him from insisting on standards. That Eskimos, of a different race and in a different climate, lend their wives is no reason why western Europeans should not retain theirs. Being a Liberal was never allowed to mean with him what it does for so many today, fostering an indolent, insolent complacency, in which everybody shall have the "right" to say there are no standards and flaunt his own lack of them; it meant assuring everybody of his freedom to work up to the topmost level, and encouraging him to test what powers he had for the climb. His was a Liberalism which, along with its intellectual clear-sightedness and human sympathy, knew the necessity for discipline;[10] it faced the fact that good habits can be made only through sustained effort of the will. He showed that the fruit of liberating thought and education is a character equipped to grapple manfully not only with the problems of politics and social science but with the more grievous ones of personal existence as well; he proved that democracy after all need not be incompatible with aristocracy. The consummation of his efforts was aptly what he had set his heart as a youth on achieving—"an air of dignity and size and grandeur."

[10] Morley was always fond of pointing out that often in countries where the force of the government is strongest felt, the inhabitants are surprisingly better natured on the whole than elsewhere. So, too, in domestic life, while he never sanctioned tyrannizing household autocrats, he did believe in a modified absolutism, as The Fortnightly once showed: "A certain austerity of parental discipline is no bad preparation for encountering the assured and inevitable austerities that nature and circumstances have in store, as we emerge from youth to fight the battles of life in earnest."

The sad loss in Morley's life, so far as posterity is concerned, is that the whole print of it was never left in his books. The vigorous mind has been set down, the unflinching will, the disdainful irony, the boldness and breadth of purpose, and the unimpeachable honesty. But where are the quiet voice, the urbane demeanor, the easy sense of humor, the slight gentle smile, the gracious sympathy, the disarming readiness to listen —in short, the charm, the magic which in person he exerted? Johnson's *Rambler*, Boswell reminds us, was not a work which the public liked, because of the permeation of his "grave and often solemn cast of thinking," so in contrast with his hearty, many-sided humanity as Boswell exhibits him to us in his biography. A similar disparity exists between Morley's durable work and his character as it was known to his friends in actual life. Important as his work is for the information it contains, and influential as it has been for its critical and historical procedure, the volumes which compose it will likely remain, in spite of the effect of some of them on a past generation, books of knowledge rather than of power, or, perhaps, books of such a singular power as to attract few readers and win few friends. The limitations of the central quality which pervades and colors them appear clearly when he is seen alongside his eminent contemporary and friend, Matthew Arnold.

In the very early 1870's, in utter disregard of the fact that his own essays back in 1865 and 1867 had been more than negligibly charged with his thought, Morley was cocky in his dismissal of Arnold, and described his criticism to Harrison as "nonsensical flummery about sweetness and light." Harrison himself laughed at Arnold as "dilly-dallying stuff" after Morley's early volume of critical miscellanies. Arnold, the older and more sober of the two, was unperturbed by several "severe attacks" made by Morley on his things and wrote calmly to his sister in 1871 of the *Fortnightly* scourge "who has certainly learnt something from me and knows it." Later, in closer contact with him and tempered by experience, Morley could acknowledge more easily Arnold's aims and form a clearer estimate of his character. In his *Recollections* he confesses that from his "Oxford days onward" he owed him much and knew it. Certainly by 1876 the two were more than respectful acquaintances, and Arnold could be delighted by Morley's relaying to him what George Sand had said to Renan about him when she saw him years before as a boy—that he looked like a young Milton traveling. In the early 'eighties Arnold thought enough of Morley's books to recommend them, and of Morley himself to address him in his letters with endearment. His affection was reciprocated; Morley made himself such a gracious friend that Arnold, though he had known him earlier through his writing as "a bitter political partisan," described him in company as "the gentlest and most charming of men." Nor was Morley a laggard in his tributes to the poet-critic. He is said to have told Arnold that in traveling he always carried along one of his volumes, which he read, before making a speech, for inspiration, and afterward, for consolation. In print, at one time, he quoted lovingly "those admirable closing lines" of the "thrice lovely *Sohrab and Rustum*," and, at another, proclaimed their author "among the foremost poets of his period, . . . quite its greatest literary critic, . . . the 'most distinguished' figure in the literature of the age and country to which he belongs." Indeed, Arnold's death, in his own admission, left a "painful void" in his life; and years after it he singled him out as one of the few men he had known who had possessed actual charm.

Remarkable in the relationship of the two men is the closeness of their minds, the more-than-coincidental similarity in numerous conclusions they reached. The standards of moral conduct which they strove to preserve are those that save the individual, as well as society, from dissolution; they prevent life from collapsing into a chaotic welter, an idiot's tale, and alone give it meaning. For both of them human relationships had sanctity, and "let us be true to one another" was a first commandment, not because the church had ordained it but because their experience had shown civilized living to be impossible without it. Even "in matters of feeling," Arnold had an instinct that he and Morley were "apt to be in sympathy," and he hesitated about accepting a government pension because he wanted to be "fortified" by Morley's opinion beforehand. In their attitudes toward a good many authors—Burke, George Sand, Macaulay, Emerson, and Tennyson—they were in agreement; and Arnold knew that in his heart, Morley, despite his preoccupation with political Liberalism, believed as sincerely as he himself did in the value of classical studies.

Equally parallel were their beliefs about the function of literature. For both of them it was the vehicle of culture; Morley's "multiplicity of sympathies and steadiness of sight" is close to Arnold's "sweetness and light." And, as has been shown, Morley developed a conception of the purpose of criticism as broad as that which Arnold described in his *The Function of Criticism at the Present Time* when he said that it ought "to create a current of true and fresh ideas" and establish an intellectual atmosphere for igniting creative minds. In some respects, however, a fair amount of Morley's journalistic criticism shows up more narrow, more insular; it has too much to do with what Arnold erringly thought should be omitted entirely— "those ulterior, political, practical considerations about ideas."[11] And *The Fortnightly Review* as an "organ of criticism" was in many ways what Arnold considered the bane of criticism in his time, an organ of "men and parties having prac-

[11] There was often, to be sure, a certain snobbishness in Arnold's holding himself aloof from what he patronizingly labeled the practical, and it was precisely this which justified Morley in feeling that his excessively "literary point of view" prevented him, in his critical analysis of certain subjects, religion, for example, from penetrating to "the heart of the matter." Yet if Arnold went too far in one direction, Morley was often inclined to be equally extreme in its opposite.

tical ends to serve." Much that Morley wrote was too polemical to live. Not that he intentionally put the stamp of partisanship on it, but simply that since it was turned out in the heat of controversy, it could not escape the tinge. Arnold made it his purpose to avoid heatedness; the militant attitude was repugnant to him.

The something in Morley harder and more austere at the core, predominates in his style. Though it more than conforms to what Arnold thought were "the needful qualities for a fit prose . . . regularity, uniformity, precision, balance," it is never winning as Arnold's was. It could be forcefully brilliant, it could attain gravity, sonority, dignity, and contain memorably striking phrases, yet it remained always formal and tense. It needed to be more pliant and flexible, more graceful, more intimate on occasion—more what he in his own person was and revealed himself to be in his letters. Arnold's prose attracts and establishes a sympathetic bond, and so do Pater's and Ruskin's, but Morley's almost never does, unless it be in the *Recollections*, where it is shortened, more economical, with something of the easiness of his conversation, and equally vivid without being so rhetorical. And if the first volume of the *Recollections* is the product of his meridian and not his decline, as has been said, then it is regrettable that he did not continue writing in that vein, which is a complete departure from the vehemence and grandness of the French studies. Here for the first time he has adopted a "quiet style." Yet it is the French studies and the miscellaneous critical essays written about the same time which are the bulk of his durable work, and their style will have to be the style by which he is judged. The man who is revealed in them will remain the man whom future readers think of and feel as John Morley.

Arnold as a critic, said Morley, was "more at home in a velvet glove." Yet the grace, the discernible humanity in Arnold make him pleasurably readable today; the sharpness of edge,

the austerity in Morley not infrequently repel. After a reading
of his criticism, one cannot erase the picture of a warrior from
one's mind. Inflamed by the doctrines of Mill, one sees him
discarding the gown of the saint for the weapons of the soldier
and girding himself for war. None of Mill's humility in the
face of Truth is in his militant declarations. Like the brothers
in David's *Oath of the Horatii*, he stands defiant and taut, on
guard to defend his vows in the cause of Liberalism. And like
them, he has his sword drawn to fight for his spiritual convictions, too. One senses that he is steeled constantly against the
tragedies, the uglinesses of life, sorrowful, to be sure, but intent on revealing no shock, no revulsion, out of contempt for
softness. There is no time for tears. He looks at death, at the
inevitable end of all existence on this earth, and holds himself
scornfully above any "shivering mood" of doubt, any "sentimental juvenilities of children crying for light," as Lucretius
held himself on his serene plane above the futilities of the
world. He strives for a limited perspective, "figures the merciless vastness of the universe of matter sweeping us headlong
through viewless space," "hears the wail of misery that is forever ascending to the deaf gods," "counts the little tale of the
years that separate us from eternal silence," and annihilates
any interest in bodies as bodies, in flesh as flesh. They are
ephemeral, and their decay must mean nothing to him except
an incidental fact in an unstoppable process, the ceaseless
operation of Nature. His somberness on occasion is like the
tone of a mediaeval sermonizer in sackcloth, or of the ascetic
Marcus Aurelius meditating on death.

For one wonders whether, like Marcus Aurelius, Morley did
not see a death's head underlying almost everything human
beings do. The Easter Meditations in the second volume of the
Recollections, or numerous passages from some of the French
studies—*Rousseau*, for example—suggest this eloquently. Is
there not in them something of the same preoccupation with

death, the same attempt to confront it and dispel its horror by looking it full in the face? At thirty-five, he had brought himself to be dispassionately candid about "the millions who come on to the earth that greets them with no smile and then stagger blindly under dull burdens for a season, and at last are shovelled silently back under the ground." Bolstered himself, he went on to proclaim that human consideration might be more widespread if more men held his own courageous, unfalsifying realization that there is no "perfect companionable bliss" in other worlds to come, but "that the bleak and horrible grave is indeed the end of our communion." It is this too-frequent mortuary cast to Morley's thinking, even in his best criticism, that is unattractive, and it is this Davidian sternness and militancy of tone that repels. What he said about Diderot, that he never wrote "as if his spirit were quite free," describes aptly the deficiency in his own work. The very temper of mind he had early placed a premium on and dedicated himself to cultivating, he succeeded in transmitting flawlessly to his pages; but, ironically, if intellectual strenuousness is their supreme distinction, it is their ineradicable detriment, too.

And so one leaves him in that attitude which he himself once described as the only admirable one, convinced that there "is no solace obtainable except that of an energetic fortitude," striding into life "not in a softly lined silken robe, but with a sharp sword and armour thrice tempered."

INDEX